George W. Ross

The School System of Ontario (Canada)

Its History and Distinctive Features

George W. Ross

The School System of Ontario (Canada)
Its History and Distinctive Features

ISBN/EAN: 9783337187378

Printed in Europe, USA, Canada, Australia, Japan

Cover: Foto ©Paul-Georg Meister /pixelio.de

More available books at **www.hansebooks.com**

INTERNATIONAL EDUCATION SERIES

THE
SCHOOL SYSTEM OF ONTARIO
(CANADA)

ITS HISTORY AND DISTINCTIVE FEATURES

BY

THE HON. GEORGE W. ROSS, LL. D.

MINISTER OF EDUCATION FOR THE PROVINCE OF ONTARIO
AUTHOR OF
THE SCHOOLS OF ENGLAND AND GERMANY
PATRIOTIC RECITATIONS FOR SCHOOLS AND COLLEGES, ETC.

NEW YORK
D. APPLETON AND COMPANY
1896

COPYRIGHT, 1896,
BY D. APPLETON AND COMPANY.

ELECTROTYPED AND PRINTED
AT THE APPLETON PRESS, U. S. A.

EDITOR'S PREFACE.

The publishers take pleasure in presenting a new volume in the fourth department of this series, that of Practice or Education as an art. This is a work on the organization and supervision of schools, and a most instructive one. After the history of educational theories and their criticism, one is prepared for a study of systematic treatises on the theory of pedagogy. Then come treatises on the art of instruction and discipline; and lastly, in our classification, works on the organization and supervision of schools.

Next after the study of school organization in the several States of our own country comes that of the colonies of Great Britain. Descended, like ourselves, from the people that invented local self-government, their solutions of the problem of popular education have in many respects the same features that we find in the United States. But, unlike our own people, these colonies have never passed through an epoch of revolution and become separate from the parental Government. From this circumstance flows a stream of results that mark considerable differences in practice.

It was natural that the people of our colonies should develop an almost morbid feeling against centralization. The true civil government is a proper balance between centralization and individualism, the central power limiting itself to doing such things only as the individual can not do so well, and in all cases helping the individual to help himself. With our phobia against centralization, there have been frequent cases in which the central Government has failed to take the initiative in matters of great public concern. The individual has in many instances been left to suffer for his feebleness where he might have been re-enforced and made strong by the social whole. The consequence has been a slower growth in that function of our Government which, in the language of the Constitution, is "to provide for the public welfare."

The British colonies in many particulars furnish instances where the central power has acted more freely and provided for the public welfare more wisely than it has done with us.

Take, in the present volume, the account of the persistent attempt to secure the best method of supervision (Chapters I and II)—an attempt crowned with success. Take the record that describes the growth of the codes of comprehensive rules and regulations for the administration of details in localities. The central power sets the standards so that the local authority can readily see the ideal and criticise for itself its own results. The individual is left free in many details of method, but must secure a certain standard of success in what he accomplishes.

We may read with interest and profit the growth of the plan for the professional training of teachers; that for school libraries, and the final substitution of town or village public libraries; that for secondary and higher education; that for the provision of good text-books;

the care for equal justice in the matter of separate schools for religious denominations; the systematic modes of procedure in selecting schoolhouse sites and in adopting plans for building that secure the best hygiene for teacher and pupil.

Throughout this volume is seen what may be done by a central power that makes a liberal appropriation of money to local authorities, but requires, as a condition, the recipient to respond by contributing an equal sum of money, and by showing to the central supervisory power results that equal the standard of requirement. It may be doubted whether there is another instance in America of so wise a use of money and supervisory power as is shown in this Province of Ontario, excepting the administration of the Peabody and Slater funds for the stimulation and nurture of education in our Southern States. The Peabody fund is worth studying as another example of wise centralization used for increasing local and individual self-help.

In proportion to the progress of our country toward an urban condition of civilization and the political subordination of the rural phase, we ourselves achieve this desirable feature of wise centralization that really and truly "provides for the public welfare," in the sense that the deep-seeing mind of Jefferson used those words. We at the same time outgrow that morbid jealousy of centralization, not fearing any longer the usurpation of our liberties, now that we have the newspaper, universal free suffrage, and a government by public opinion.

The difference between a well-balanced civil government and socialism is as well marked as the difference between mere individualism and anarchy; for, while the civil state helps the locality or the individual only where it can increase local or individual self-help, or where the interest of the social whole is subserved by it, socialism does the deed for the individual and destroys his power of self-help altogether. It assumes all directive power—all power of initiative. The civil government of the Anglo-Saxon finds the true balance between central and local powers where each re-enforces the other.

The school system at home in Great Britain is still complicated with questions of caste, and not so instructive to us or so easily understood as the school systems of the English colonies.

W. T. HARRIS.

WASHINGTON, *March 1, 1896.*

AUTHOR'S PREFACE.

EVERY school system has its own distinctive features. An ideal organization is scarcely possible in any case. The living forces which shape and mould the political institutions of a people also shape and mould its educational institutions, so that any system, to be successful, must adapt itself to social and local conditions. The school system described in the following pages is the evolution of the best thought of different Legislatures, aided and directed by the judgment of men who gave a lifetime to the task of adapting broad principles of organization and pedagogy to the wants and aspirations of the people for whom it was designed. Briefly summarized its chief characteristics are as follows:

1. It is an organized whole, beginning with the kindergarten and ending with the university.

2. It provides free education to all persons under twenty-one years of age.

3. It graduates the courses of study from the kindergarten to the university, so as to avoid waste of time on the part of the pupils and waste of teaching power on the part of the teachers.

4. It provides a trained teacher for every school, aided by public money.

5. It furnishes a uniform standard of examination for every teacher, according to his rank.

6. It protects children against the selfishness or neglect of parents and guardians, by making attendance at school compulsory.

7. It secures trustees against the incapacity of teachers by a rigorous system of examination and inspection.

8. It protects education from the caprice of public opinion by the appointment of inspectors during pleasure, and by the election of trustees for a lengthened term of service.

9. It secures economy and uniformity in text-books by placing their publication in the hands of a central provincial authority.

10. It permits the establishment of separate schools for Roman Catholics subject to the same standards of efficiency as the public schools.

To those who are concerned in the administration of schools it is always an advantage to know what methods are adopted in other countries for securing the co-operation of the public and promoting the efficiency of educational effort. In order that the reader might be able to study the school system of Ontario, as at present organized, full details have been given of its different departments. In preserving the continuity of the statement, repetition in some cases was unavoidable. To be concise, it was necessary to omit minor matters of detail. It is hoped, however, that the statement, as a whole, will enable the intelligent reader to understand reasonably well the various features of the school system which it has been the object of the author to unfold.

GEORGE W. ROSS.

EDUCATION DEPARTMENT, TORONTO, *January 2, 1896.*

TABLE OF CONTENTS.

	PAGE
Editor's Preface	v
Author's Preface	ix

CHAPTER I.
HISTORICAL REVIEW OF THE SCHOOL SYSTEM OF ONTARIO.

Recommendation of Governor Simcoe.—Appropriation of lands for school purposes.—Public-Schools Act of 1807.—Elementary-Schools Act, 1816.—The Act of 1824.—The Act of 1841.—Germ of Separate-Schools Act.—Act of 1843.—Office of chief superintendent.—Appointment of Dr. Ryerson.—Dr. Ryerson's report on foreign schools.—The Act of 1846.—Establishment of school libraries.—Appointment of county inspectors.—Appointment of a Minister of Education . 1

CHAPTER II.
ORGANIZATION OF PUBLIC SCHOOLS.

Minister head of the Education Department.—Constitution, jurisdiction, and power of the Education Department.—Powers of the Minister of Education.—Public schools, how organized.—Government of rural schools.—Duties of trustees.—Township boards.—School assessments.—Trustees of urban schools.—Industrial schools 24

CHAPTER III.
SCHOOL SITES, PREMISES, AND PUPILS.

Law regarding school sites.—Schoolhouses, school furniture, and equipment.—Duties of pupils.—Departmental regulations *re* pupils.—Sanitary protection of 43

CHAPTER IV.

COURSE OF STUDY IN PUBLIC SCHOOLS.

Reading. — Spelling. — Writing. — Language lessons. — Geography.—History.—Drawing.—Physiology and temperance.—Literature.—Music.—Drill and calisthenics.—Moral and religious instruction.—Reviews and recitations.—Optional subjects.—Dual languages 56

CHAPTER V.

TEACHERS AND THEIR QUALIFICATIONS.

Qualification of teachers.—Subjects of third-class standing.—Subjects of second-class standing.—Subjects of first-class standing.—Specialists' certificates.—Preparation of examination papers.—Mode of conducting examinations.—Duties of candidates.—Duties of presiding examiners.—Reading answer papers 70

CHAPTER VI.

TRAINING OF TEACHERS.

County model schools.—Course of study in.—Final examinations of.—Normal schools.—Organization of normal schools.—Course of study in.—Examinations, how. conducted.—Kindergarten teachers.— Normal Training College.— Courses of study and text-books.—Teaching staff.—Specialists.—Teachers' institutes 80

CHAPTER VII.

HIGH SCHOOLS AND COLLEGIATE INSTITUTES.

Historical sketch. — Acts of 1807, 1841, 1853, 1865. — High schools, how established.—Duties and powers of trustees.—Sites and buildings.—How sustained.—Fees.—Course of study. — Physical culture. — Qualification of teachers.— Upper Canada College 111

CHAPTER VIII.

INSPECTION OF SCHOOLS AND RELIGIOUS INSTRUCTION.

PAGE

Qualification of inspectors.—Duties of public-school inspectors.—High-school inspection.—Inspection of teachers' institutes.—Inspection of model schools.—Religious instruction.—Departmental regulations 128

CHAPTER IX.

DENOMINATIONAL SCHOOLS.

Established under the Act of 1841.—Continued in 1843.—Acts of 1852, 1855, 1863.—Organization of Roman Catholic separate schools.—Who are separate-school supporters.—Separate schools, how sustained.—Separate-school teachers.—Course of study, text-books, and inspection.—Protestant separate schools.—Coloured separate schools 140

CHAPTER X.

SCHOOL LIBRARIES, PUBLIC LIBRARIES, AND TEXT-BOOKS.

Historical Sketch.—Mechanics' institutes.—Free Libraries Act, 1882.—Government aid.—Regulations respecting public libraries.—Evening classes in art schools.—Text-books.—One text-book in each subject.—Text-books, how prepared.—How published 156

CHAPTER XI.

THE PROVINCIAL UNIVERSITY.

Historical sketch.—The Act of 1837.—The Act of 1849.—The Act of 1853.—The Act of 1873.—The Federation Act, 1887.—Government of the university.—Faculty, how appointed.—The Senate.—Matriculation.—Course of study.—Faculty of medicine.—Affiliated universities and colleges.—The library.—Gymnasium.—Discipline.—College residence.—The School of Science 173

CHAPTER XII.

GROWTH OF THE ONTARIO SCHOOL SYSTEM.

Returns of 1844.—Pupils in advanced subjects.—Number of trained teachers.—Salaries of teachers.—Cost of public schools.—Growth of separate schools.—Growth of high schools.—Percentages in different subjects.—Salaries of masters.—County model schools and normal schools.—Growth of public libraries.—Results of Arbor Day.—Attendance at the provincial university 188

APPENDIX.

Report on the sanitary condition of rural schools . . . 198

THE SCHOOL SYSTEM OF ONTARIO (CANADA).

CHAPTER I.

HISTORICAL REVIEW OF THE SCHOOL SYSTEM OF ONTARIO.

BY an act known as the Constitutional Act of 1791, the Imperial House of Commons divided the British possessions in America into two provinces to be known as Upper and Lower Canada, which names they retained until all the British provinces were united by the British North America Act of 1867 as the Dominion of Canada. Since that time Lower Canada has been known by the name of Quebec, and Upper Canada by the name of Ontario. To avoid confusion, it is proposed to use the name " Ontario " instead of " Upper Canada " in the historical narrative that follows.

The Province of Ontario contains an area of 219,650 square miles, with a population of 2,114,321, or about the same population as the State of Massachusetts. In area it is larger by 50,000 square miles than the nine States generally described as the North Atlantic States of the American Republic, viz., Maine, New Hampshire, Vermont, Massachusetts, Rhode Island, Connecticut, New

York, New Jersey, and Pennsylvania. There is no record of the population of Ontario at the date of the Constitutional Act of 1791; in 1806, however, its population is stated as being 70,718, and in 1814 as 95,000.

The early settlers of Ontario were mainly immigrants from the British Islands and refugees from the United States called United Empire Loyalists, because they disapproved of the Revolution which led to the separation of the North American colonies from Great Britain.

On the 11th of November, 1791, Lieutenant-Governor J. Graves Simcoe, the first Governor of Ontario, arrived in Quebec, and on the 17th of September, 1792, the first Legislature of Upper Canada assembled at Newark, a little village on the Niagara River about seven miles below the Falls, now known as Niagara. By the act of the Imperial Parliament, under which this Legislature was convened, the people of Ontario, through a Parliament of their own choice, had the right to legislate with regard to all matters which concerned the development of the country and the welfare of the people educationally and socially.

On Simcoe's nomination to his office as Governor, he evidently revolved in his mind how best he could secure a solid foundation for the government and institutions of the youthful colony intrusted to his care. Religion and education were his watchwords. The form in which he wished them introduced into the new province was, the first in the person of a chief ecclesiastic, and the other as an endowed university. "The former was to inculcate in all ranks and descriptions of people a sober, industrious, religious, and conscientious spirit, which shall be the best security that a government can have for its own internal preservation. The latter, with the liberal education which it would afford, would be most useful to inculcate just principles, habits, and manners into the rising generation."

These views Governor Simcoe impressed upon the imperial authorities and upon the dignitaries of the Church of England in a correspondence extending over several years. In a letter addressed to the Duke of Portland, dated July 20, 1796, he urged " the erection and endowment of a university, from which more than from any other source, a grateful attachment to his Majesty, morality, and religion will be fostered and take root throughout the whole province."

Governor Simcoe, on account of ill health, was relieved of his duties in August, 1796, but, as a result of his influence upon the public opinion of the country, the Legislature on the 1st of July, 1797, memorialized the British Government " to set apart certain portions of the waste land of the Crown as a fund for the establishment and support of a respectable grammar school in each district of the province, and also of a college or a university for the instruction of the youth in the different branches of liberal knowledge."

The Imperial Government having given its consent, the Executive Council for the province took the matter up, and on the 1st of December, 1798, recommended the establishment of a grammar school in each of the four districts into which the province was divided, viz., at Cornwall, Kingston, Newark, and Sandwich, but owing to the limited revenues at their disposal it was decided that only the schools at Kingston and Newark should be opened at once.* They recommended that the university

---

* These schools were not opened till after the passage of the Public-School Act of 1807.

should be established at the town of York, now called Toronto, and that 500,000 acres of the wild lands of the province should be set apart, from the sale of which a sufficient endowment would be obtained to provide for the necessary expenses of the schools and the university.

The Legislature had as yet, however, taken no steps for the organization of an elementary school system for the province, and no schools of any kind were in existence except such as were maintained by the voluntary contributions of the people.

Public Schools, Act of 1807.—Although petitions had been presented from time to time, and bills of various kinds submitted for the organization of a system both of primary and secondary education, it was not until the year 1807 that any progress was made. In that year an act was passed establishing eight public schools in the province. This act is the germ of the act now in force with regard to secondary education, from which the Province of Ontario has derived such incalculable advantages. By this act $400 were set apart for the payment of the salary of a teacher for each school. Five trustees were to be appointed by the Lieutenant-Governor of the Province for each district, whose duty it was to "nominate a fit and discreet person as a teacher, and to examine into the moral character, learning, and capacity of such person so nominated, and, being satisfied with the moral character, learning, and capacity of such person," to recommend him for appointment by the Lieutenant-Governor. The trustees were to have the power of dismissing the teacher if his moral character was unsatisfactory, or if he was unfit for his duties, and to nominate another for the approval of the Lieutenant-Governor. The trustees had authority to make such rules and regulations for the good government and management of the school with respect to teachers and scholars as in their discretion they deemed expedient. The duration of this act was first limited to four years, but afterward this limitation was withdrawn, and the act amended from year to year as public opinion demanded. Its provisions, as modified during the last eighty years, are fully considered in a subsequent chapter.

Elementary Schools, Act of 1816.—Having secured the establishment of eight public schools in the province with a reasonable provision for their maintenance, the Legislative Assembly next addressed itself to the duty of providing elementary schools for the great mass of the people. It was not until the year 1816 that these efforts were crowned with success. The act passed for this purpose was approved by the Lieutenant-Governor on the 1st of April of that year, and was entitled "An Act granting to his Majesty a sum of money to be applied to the use of common schools, and to provide for the organization of said common schools." The principal provisions of this act are:

1. The appropriation of $24,000 to be divided as the Lieutenant-Governor might direct among such schools as were established according to law, but in no case was any school to receive more than $100.

2. The inhabitants of the town, township, village, or place concerned were authorized to meet in public assembly, and so soon as they had erected a suitable schoolhouse and were able to show that twenty children were likely to attend the same, they were to appoint three fit and discreet persons to act as trustees of the said school, with authority to appoint a teacher.

3. The qualifications of the teacher were determined

by the trustees, as they, and they alone, had the power and authority to examine into his moral character and capacity for the duties of his office. Every teacher appointed must be a British subject either by birth or naturalization. No teacher could be removed by the trustees without the approval of the Board of Education having supervision for the district in which the school was situated.

4. The trustees were authorized to make such rules and regulations for the good government of their respective schools, both with regard to teachers and pupils, as they deemed expedient. They were to report to the district board with regard to the text-books to be used in their schools, and the rules and regulations which they had made for the government of the school, all of which were subject to the approval of the district board. The moneys appropriated by the Legislature were to be apportioned to the teachers of the several schools yearly or half-yearly, as might be directed by the trustees, in proportion to the number of scholars in attendance, provided the number was not less than twenty.

5. The Lieutenant-Governor was authorized to appoint a Board of Education for each of the eight districts into which the province was divided, to be composed of five discreet persons who had authority to superintend the schools established under the act.

6. The Board of Education for the district was authorized to expend a sum not exceeding $400 of the amount appropriated to the district for the purchase of proper books for the use of the schools, and to distribute those books among them as was considered expedient.

Special Features.—Several features of this early act

are noteworthy, viz. : 1. The trustees were elected by a majority of the inhabitants of the district, irrespective of all property qualification, and were the sole judges of the fitness of the teacher for the duties of his office. The teacher's tenure of office was more secure in those early days than it is now, as no teacher could be dismissed except with the approval of the Board of Education for the district. 2. The school grant was based upon the attendance of the pupils, but no grant was to be paid unless there were at least twenty in attendance. 3. The trustees had the right to select text-books for the use of pupils, and to make regulations for the government of the school, subject to the approval of the District Board of Education. 4. No provision was made for levying rates upon property for the maintenance of the school. All sums required over and above the Government grant had to be raised by voluntary contributions. 5. There was no provision for inspection or supervision; the Boards of Education for the districts had the right to refuse their assent to the regulations made for the government of the school, and in that way promote uniformity of management. They depended, however, for all the information by which they were to be guided upon the reports of the trustees. 6. The schools were to be known as common schools, a name which in 1871 was changed to public schools.

The School Act of 1816 contained but sixteen sections, and was the first attempt of the Legislature of Ontario to provide for the educational wants of the whole people of the province, and, elementary though it was, it was a statutory recognition of the right of the people, under the direction of an act of Parliament, to provide for the education of their children. It is true that the teachers appointed by the trustees might not have been in all cases entitled to rank as members of a learned profession, as we now understand the term. They were not, however, devoid of scholarship, many of them having received a liberal education in the schools of their native land. As a rule, the curriculum was limited to reading, writing, and arithmetic, with a moderate drill in British history and the geography of the world, so far as then known. The log schoolhouse, with its rude, primitive accommodation, was, in the fullest sense of the term, the people's university, and, except in the towns and villages, was the only school available to the great majority of the people.

The Act of 1824.—The next important amendment to the Common-Schools Act of 1816 was an act approved by the Legislative Assembly on the 19th day of January, 1824. It has already been noted that in each of the eight districts into which the province was divided the Lieutenant-Governor was authorized to appoint, and did appoint, a Board of Education having authority to appropriate the moneys granted by the Legislature, and in a general way to exercise a limited control over the schools with regard to management and discipline. In 1824 provision was made for the appointment of a general Board of Education for the whole province. This board was appointed by the Lieutenant-Governor, and in the first instance consisted of the Rev. John Strachan, D. D., chairman; the Hon. Joseph Wells, a member of the Legislative Council; the Hon. George H. Markland, also a member of the Legislative Council; the Rev. Robert Addison, John Beverly Robinson, Attorney-General, and Thomas Ridout, Surveyor-General. This board afterwards developed into a Council of Public Instruction in the year 1850, with powers to prescribe text-books, courses of study for common and grammar schools, qualifications of teachers, etc., but was abolished in 1876 when the schools of the province were placed under a Minister of Education.

It appears that the Legislative Assembly was impressed with the necessity for promoting the " moral and religious instruction of the more indigent and remote settlements in the several districts throughout the province," and that accordingly the sum of $600, in addition to the amounts voted for common schools, was granted for the encouragement of Sunday schools. This sum was placed at the disposition of the Board of Education for the province, to be by it laid out and expended for the purchasing of books and tracts designed to afford moral and religious instruction, such books and tracts to be distributed in equal proportions among the several District Boards of Education throughout the province. This would give $75 for the moral and religious education of the pupils of each district; and as there were over two hundred schools in the province at that time, the appropriation to each must have been exceedingly small. It showed, however, the sympathy of the Legislature with the moral and religious education of the people.

Another and more important provision was made in the act with respect to the qualifications of the teacher. By the Act of 1816 the trustees were authorized to examine the teacher they proposed to employ, and to satisfy themselves as to his fitness mentally and morally. By the Act of 1824 this duty was transferred to the Board of Education for the district, and no school could receive any portion of the public grant unless the teacher held a certificate signed by at least one member of the district board. There were in all at this time eleven district boards in the province.

The Act of 1841.—In 1841 the Provinces of Upper and Lower Canada (Ontario and Quebec) were united under one Legislature or Parliament, and among the subjects receiving the early attention of the Legislature, education appears to have been most earnestly considered. On the 18th of September, 1841, an act was passed of a somewhat comprehensive character, which showed the great interest taken by the people in the development of a system of elementary schools.

1. It was provided that a permanent fund should be established in each township and parish in the province (Ontario and Quebec were then called the Province of Canada), consisting of such money as might accrue from the sale of lands appropriated by the Legislature or be in any other way provided for the maintenance of common schools.

2. The grant for education was increased to $200,000 —a very liberal sum, considering the resources and population of the country at that time.

3. Authority was taken for the appointment of a Chief Superintendent of Education, who was to hold office during pleasure, at a salary of $3,000.

4. Municipal Councils were empowered to raise by assessment such sums of money for school purposes as would be at least equivalent to the amount appropriated by the Legislature for the maintenance of each school.

5. The district boards of trustees appointed by the Lieutenant-Governor in Council under the Act of 1807 were abolished, and the Municipal Council for the district was constituted the Board of Education of such district.

6. The Municipal Council, as the Board of Education for the district, was authorized to divide the several townships in their districts into school sections and to assess the inhabitants to the extent of $200 for the erection of a schoolhouse in each section where none existed, and to appropriate a sum of $40 for the purchase of such books as might be recommended by the school commissioners for the district.

7. Five persons were to be appointed for each township, or parish to be known as Common-School Commissioners, whose duty it was to select school sites, superintend the building of schoolhouses, appoint teachers, regulate the course of study in each school, select textbooks and make rules for the conduct of the schools, hear and settle complaints, visit each school in their township at least once a month by one or more of their number, relieve poor persons not exceeding ten from the payment of school fees for the education of their children, and report their proceedings to the Municipal Council before the close of the year in the form furnished by the Superintendent of Education.

8. A monthly fee of twenty-five cents was to be paid by each pupil attending the school, in addition to the rates which might be levied by assessment for school purposes. No public moneys were to be paid to any school attended by less than fifteen children, and unless the ratepayers raised a sum equal to the Government grant.

9. The religious minority, whether Protestant or Catholic, in any township or parish who dissented from the proceedings of the school commissioners of any parish had the right of signifying their dissent in writing to the clerk of the Municipal Council, and, on submitting the names of persons to act for them as trustees, to establish

common schools on their own behalf. The trustees so appointed were to have the authority and be subject to the obligations and liabilities of ordinary school commissioners. They were to be subject to the "visitation, condition, rules, and obligations provided with reference to other common schools, and to receive from the municipal treasurer the due appropriation according to the number of pupils and the moneys appropriated by law, and raised by assessment for the support of common schools." Such moneys were to be paid to them upon the order of their own trustees.

A few things in this act are noteworthy: 1. Provision was made for the appointment of a Chief Superintendent for the whole province. As the Act of 1841 applied to both Ontario and Quebec, the jurisdiction of the Chief Superintendent, in this case, would apply to both provinces. 2. The Legislature for the first time declared by statute that the property of the people was held in trust for the education of the people, as, in addition to the large grants given directly by the Legislature for common-school education, the school commissioners were authorized to tax the inhabitants for the maintenance of schools; and although a monthly fee of twenty-five cents was still chargeable upon pupils, a great advance had been made toward free schools, the evident goal of the early educational leaders of the province. 3. Township Boards of Trustees called school commissioners, elected by the people, were intrusted with all matters affecting common schools in each township or parish. 4. The principle of separate schools for Roman Catholics and Protestants, respectively, was admitted for the first time by statute. 5. As all reports had to be made to the Chief Superintendent, and as he was authorized to visit the schools and ascertain their standing for himself, it was evidently the desire of the Legislature to secure greater uniformity in the administration of the schools.*

The Act of 1843.—The apathy shown by Parliament hitherto in dealing with educational matters had now given place to great activity, and in the session of 1843 an act was passed involving many changes of great importance to the country. On account of the dissimilarity in race and religion of the people of Ontario and Quebec, it was found difficult, if not impossible, to meet the peculiar conditions of each province by a common system of education. Accordingly, the Act of 1841 was repealed, and the schools of the two provinces were organized in a manner more in harmony with the wishes of the people of each province. The provisions of the Act of 1843, as applicable to Ontario only concern us.

1. The office of Chief Superintendent was abolished, and the member of the Government occupying the position of Provincial Secretary was appointed Chief Superintendent of Education for the Province of Ontario. The Governor of the province was invested with authority to appoint an assistant superintendent, who was to act in all things under the direction of the Provincial Secretary, as his chief.

2. County Councils were authorized to appoint a superintendent for their respective counties, and every city, town, and township was authorized to appoint a

---

* On the 11th of May, 1842, Vice-Chancellor Jameson was appointed Chief Superintendent of Education for Ontario and Quebec, and the Rev. Robert Murray, a minister of the Church of Scotland at Oakville, was appointed Assistant Superintendent under this act. He held office for about two years, and was afterward appointed Professor of Mathematics in the University of Toronto.

superintendent who was to act under the direction of the county superintendent. These officers all held office during pleasure.

3. The city, town, and township superintendents were authorized to divide the districts under their jurisdictions as far as might be necessary, into school sections, to visit the schools under their care at least once a year, to examine teachers as to their moral character, learning, and ability, and to grant them certificates as teachers valid for one year.

4. By the adoption of a system of reports with regard to the standing of children, a certain degree of uniformity was secured in the administration of the schools.

5. The government of the school sections by school commissioners was abolished, and the provisions of the Act of 1824 for the election of three trustees were reverted to. The trustees so elected were to have the right to appoint teachers, fix their salaries, regulate the course of study and the books to be used therein, and generally all matters affecting discipline and school management. All plans for the erection or alteration of schoolhouses were subject to the approval of the Municipal Council in the city, town, or township in which the school was situated.

6. A conscience clause for the first time appears in the statute to the effect that "no child shall be required to read or study in or from any religious book, or to join in any exercise of devotion or religion that shall be objected to by his or her guardian."

7. Separate schools for the minority were continued. It was provided that wherever the teacher of a school happened to be a Roman Catholic, the Protestant inhabitants had the right to establish a school with a teacher of their own religious persuasion, upon the

application of ten or more resident freeholders or householders. A similar privilege was allowed to Roman Catholics. Schools established under these conditions were to be entitled to their share of the Government grant the same as other schools established under the act, subject to the same visitations, conditions, rules, and obligations as other common schools.

8. County Councils were authorized to levy the sum of $800 upon the taxpayers of the county for the establishment of a model school. The purpose of this model school is not clear; it would appear, however, to be intended for the training of teachers, and remained until 1877 a dead letter.

9. The establishment of a normal school for the province was anticipated by proposing certain regulations with regard to its administration as soon as it was put into operation.

Dr. Ryerson appointed Chief Superintendent.—On the appointment of Mr. Murray to the professorship of Mathematics in the University of Toronto in 1844, the Rev. Egerton Ryerson, better known as Dr. Ryerson, who had for many years actively identified himself with the educational movements of the province, was appointed Assistant Superintendent,* and directed by Lord Metcalfe, who was then Governor of the province, to visit the schools of Great Britain and the Continent with a view "to devise such measures as may be necessary to provide proper school books, to establish the most efficient system of instruction, to elevate the character of both teachers and schools, and to encourage every plan

---

* Dr. Ryerson was appointed Chief Superintendent under the Act of 1850, and the office of assistant abolished.

and effort to educate and improve the youthful mind of the country."

Dr. Ryerson devoted upward of a year to the duty thus imposed upon him, and extended his inquiries into the dominions of nearly twenty governments, among them Prussia, Denmark, Sweden, Holland, Belgium, France, Switzerland, Austria, and Great Britain. On his return he submitted a very elaborate report on the school systems of the schools he visited, and recommended the establishment in the province of—

1. A system of graduated schools composed of elementary, model, grammar schools, and colleges. The elementary schools were intended to correspond to what were then called the common schools of Ontario and the primary schools of France and Prussia; the model schools were to be industrial or real or trade schools, like the polytechnic schools of Vienna and Paris, though on a smaller scale, or like the real or trade schools of Prussia; the grammar schools were to occupy the position and fulfil the functions of the French communal schools or royal colleges, and the Prussian burgher schools and gymnasia—the whole superstructure to be crowned by a provincial university or universities.

"Under such an organization," Dr. Ryerson says, "the same principles and spirit would pervade the entire system, from the primary schools up to the university; the basis of education in the elementary schools would be the same for the whole community—at least so far as governmental provisions and regulations are concerned—not interfering with private schools or taking them into account; but as soon as the pupils would advance to the limits of the instruction provided for all, then those whose parents or guardians could no longer dispense with their services would enter life with a sound elementary education; those whose parents might be able and disposed would proceed, some to the *Real* school to prepare for the business of a farmer, an architect, an engineer, a manufacturer, or mechanic, and others to the grammar school to prepare for the university and the profession."

" In the carrying out and completion of such a system the courses of instruction in each class of schools would be prescribed, as also the qualifications for admission into each of them, above the primary schools; each school would occupy its appropriate place, and each teacher would have his appropriate work; and no man in one and the same school, and on one and the same day, would be found making the absurd and abortive attempt of teaching the a, b, c's, reading, spelling, writing, arithmetic, grammar, geography (in all their gradations), together with Latin, Greek, and mathematics."

The Act of 1846.—Acting very largely upon the recommendations of Dr. Ryerson's report, the Legislature of Ontario, on the 23d of May, 1846, repealed the Act of 1843, and substituted for it a new act containing the following important provisions:

1. The Provincial Secretary was no longer to be regarded as Chief Superintendent of Schools. The duties of his office were to be discharged by a person appointed by the Governor of the province, at a salary of $2,000, with such assistants as might be from time to time required. The Chief Superintendent was to be subject to such orders and directions as he might receive from time to time from the Governor of the province. His duties were to see that the appropriation made by the Legislature for school purposes was properly distributed, to pre-

pare suitable forms and regulations for school reports, to decide upon all complaints that might arise with regard to the school law, to provide uniform and approved text-books in all the forms, to recommend suitable plans for schoolhouses, suitable books for school libraries, and to have the supervision of the normal school as soon as established.

2. Provision was made for the appointment of a Board of Education, to consist of not more than seven persons (the Chief Superintendent being a member *ex officio*). This board was to hold office during pleasure. Although the duties of the board were mainly advisory, it was vested with the power to select a site for a normal school for Ontario, and to make such rules and regulations as might be necessary for its government and for the admission of pupils. The board had also authority to examine and recommend or disapprove of all books, plans, or forms which might be submitted for use in any school.

3. The sum of $7,000 was appropriated for the purpose of procuring and furnishing suitable buildings for a normal school, and an equal sum for the payment of the salaries of teachers and the contingent expenses of the school.

4. District or county superintendents were continued, with the power to certify to the qualifications of teachers, as under the Act of 1841; and as no mention is made of city, town, or township superintendents, it is presumed that they were by this act abolished.

5. Clergymen of all denominations having pastoral charge within the city, town, or township in which the school is situated, judges, justices of the peace, and municipal councils, were constituted statutory visitors of the school, with a right to examine into the progress of the

pupils, and give such advice to the teacher as they might deem expedient. Such visitors, at a meeting called for the purpose, or any two of them, were authorized to certify as to the qualifications of candidates for a teacher's certificate, but such certificate was to be valid for only one year.

6. The office of school trustee as in the Act of 1843 was continued, as was also the monthly fees of pupils. Their power, however, to make regulations for the government and discipline of the school was withdrawn, such power having been vested in the Chief Superintendent.

7. The conscience clause and the clause in the act with regard to separate schools were continued.

8. Teachers' certificates were, for the first time in the history of the province, divided into three classes, first, second, and third.

The Act of 1850.—Under the Act of 1850 provision was made for—

1. The election of two trustees for each ward into which any city or town was divided for municipal purposes, and for the retirement of half of their number annually. In rural schools—i. e., schools situated in townships—provision was made for the retirement of one trustee annually. The intention of this was to secure greater continuity in the office of school trustee.

2. County councils were authorized to appoint a superintendent for the whole county, providing his jurisdiction was limited to one hundred schools, or a local superintendent for each township in the county. Each superintendent was to receive a fee of four dollars for every school under his jurisdiction.

3. Trustees of cities and towns were authorized to

appoint a superintendent with the same powers as a local superintendent appointed by the County Council.

4. A Board of Public Instruction was to be appointed for each county, to consist of county grammar-school trustees and the local superintendent of each township. The duty of this board was to grant certificates to teachers of common schools, to recommend the text-books to be used in the public schools, and to promote the establishment of public libraries. Local superintendents were, in addition, to visit every school within their jurisdiction at least once a quarter, to examine the pupils, to report upon the character and condition of the building and premises, and to deliver one public lecture in each school section on some subject "connected with the objects, plans, and means of education."

5. The office of Chief Superintendent was continued, and provision made for the appointment of a deputy, to act in his absence. The persons appointed as a Board of Education under the previous act were to be known as the Council of Public Instruction, and their number increased to nine.

6. Authority was given to the Chief Superintendent to appoint proper persons to conduct Teachers' Institutes for the purpose of "elevating the profession of schoolteaching and promoting its usefulness."

7. The sum of $12,000 was appropriated for the establishment and support of school libraries, and $4,000 for the payment of the expenses of teachers in training at the Provincial Normal School.

8. The certificates obtained by teachers who attended the normal school were made valid in any part of the province.

9. The most important change, however, effected in the Act of 1850, was the permission given by the freeholders

and householders of any school section to determine whether the school should be maintained by a monthly fee upon the pupils in attendance in addition to a tax upon the ratable property of the section, or whether all rate bills should be abolished and the schools declared free. The effect of this option was to lead to the gradual adoption of free schools by the people of the province, so that in 1871, the next period at which important legislation was passed by the Provincial Parliament, the schools were declared free by statute. As a matter of fact, however, the people, of their own motion, had already abolished fees in all the schools of the province except in about three hundred.

The School Act of 1871.—The School Act of 1871 marks an important era in the educational legislation of the province.

1. It provided that the common schools should thereafter be known as public schools, and that every school should be a free school by law, thus abolishing all rate bills and fees upon pupils. The trustees of public schools in cities, towns, and villages were allowed to exact a fee of not more than twenty cents per month on every pupil for the purpose of providing for the text-books, stationery, and other school supplies. By the same act, grammar schools were to be known thereafter as high schools and collegiate institutes. By collegiate institute was meant a high school with a larger staff of teachers, and with better facilities as to accommodation and equipment for the highest kind of secondary education.

2. Compulsory attendance at school was for the first time required for at least four months in each year, with power given to a magistrate to impose reasonable penalties upon parents who violated the law.

3. The office of local superintendent was abolished, and provision made for the appointment of county inspectors, who were to be appointed by county councils or the trustees of cities and towns from among those who were declared to be qualified by the Council of Public Instruction. No inspector was to have charge of more than one hundred and twenty schools or less than fifty, except in counties where the French or German language was the common or prevailing language; in that case an inspector might have charge of any number of schools not less than forty. Inspectors were appointed during pleasure, subject to dismissal by the Municipal Council or the trustees appointing them, or by the Lieutenant-Governor for misconduct or inefficiency. Their powers were similar to those of local superintendents under the Act of 1850, and their remuneration was fixed at a minimum of ten dollars per school.

4. Municipal councils and boards of trustees in cities were authorized to appoint boards of examiners for determining the qualifications of teachers.

5. The Council of Public Instruction was continued, and authorized to prepare examination papers on which candidates for a teacher's certificate were to be examined. The Council was also authorized to prepare a course of studies for public schools and for the training of teachers, to select text-books, and to make regulations for the government and administration of public and high schools.

6. A board of examiners was constituted for the admission of pupils to high schools, and a course of study outlined by the Council of Public Instruction.

7. An annual tax of four dollars was imposed upon every male teacher for the purpose of establishing a fund for teachers who had become disabled in the profession.

Female teachers were allowed voluntarily to contribute to this fund. This provision of the act was repealed in 1885, so far as teachers entering the profession after the 1st of July, 1886, were concerned. Those who had contributed up to that time were permitted to share in the benefits of the Act of 1871 by continuing the annual fee of four dollars.

The Act of 1876.—The only provision of the Act of 1876 which it is necessary to mention here is that which abolished the office of Chief Superintendent, and constituted the Executive Council—i. e., the members of the Executive Government of the Province—the Education Department. The head of the Education Department was by this act designated Minister of Education; the functions of the Council of Public Instruction devolved upon the Education Department, and the duties of Chief Superintendent upon the Minister of Education.

To mention the various amendments made to the school act from 1876 down to the present time (1896) would unnecessarily encumber the narrative, particularly as the evolution of the public-school system of Ontario, so far as its general principles are concerned, was completed by the Act of 1876.

In the following chapters the law respecting the public-school system of Ontario, as at present established, is considered in detail.

CHAPTER II.

ORGANIZATION OF PUBLIC SCHOOLS.

THE Dominion of Canada being under a federal form of government, its legislative powers are divided between the central authority, representing the whole country, and the provinces, representing interests of a more local character. Education is regarded as belonging to the latter class, and is under the control of the provincial Legislatures.*

In Ontario the school system consists of public schools (including kindergartens), high schools, and collegiate institutes, and a provincial university, with separate schools, under conditions hereafter stated, for Protestants, Roman Catholics, and colored people. The whole system is organically connected by means of courses of study and examinations conducted by the Department of Education. The head of the department is known as Minister of Education.

---

* As separate schools for Roman Catholics and Protestants existed in the Provinces of Ontario and Quebec when they became confederated with the other provinces, the Central Government— that is, the Government of Canada—was empowered to interfere in case any legislation was passed by the provinces that prejudicially affected any rights which the religious minority enjoyed at the time of union (1867). With this limitation, the provincial Legislatures are at liberty to promote the education of the people along whatever lines they consider most expedient.

Minister of Education.—The Minister of Education is a member of the Executive Government of the province, with a seat in Parliament, and represents necessarily the political party for the time being having control of the government of the province. He is liable to dismissal at any time, according to British usages, by the Lieutenant-Governor. Should he be defeated in a general election, it might be necessary for him to retire from office ; and should his party be defeated, his place would be filled by a representative of the successful party. As a general election takes place every four years, it is possible, even were the continuity of the office not broken in any other way, that the Minister of Education might be changed quadrennially.

To place the education of the people and all that it involves under the direct control of a political head was regarded by many as a very dangerous experiment. It was feared that it would lead to undue political influence in educational matters, to temporizing with sound principles of education, to needless attention to the clamours of the proletariat, to the postponement of necessary reforms from a fear of political irritation, and to the use of the patronage in the hands of the department without a proper regard to the educational interests of the public. These are dangers, however, that are incident to the administration of every department of government under democratic institutions, and unless the electorate exercise that eternal vigilance which is the price of liberty, any department of the public service is likely to be made subservient to the ambition of its head and of the party politically dominant for the time being.

No hard-and-fast rule can be laid down as to the relative value of government by a responsible minister and government by a bureaucracy. Under a Chief Superintendent of Education the school system of Ontario was well administered. It was progressive as to educational ideals, and it adapted itself with reasonable readiness to the growth of public sentiments and the wants of the people. It is important, however, to remember that Dr. Ryerson, who filled the office of Chief Superintendent for thirty years, and who was exceptionally well qualified to estimate its strength and weakness, recommended the change from an irresponsible chief to that of a Minister of Education, with a seat in Parliament and directly amenable to that public opinion which, under the Constitution, expresses itself in the representative assemblies of the country. In a letter addressed to the Government as far back as 1868, in which he asked to be relieved of his official duties as Chief Superintendent, Dr. Ryerson said : " Our system of public instruction has acquired such gigantic dimensions, and the network of its operations so pervades every municipality of the land and is so interwoven with our municipal and judicial systems of government, that I think its administration should now be vested in a responsible minister of the Crown, with a seat in Parliament; and that I should not stand in the way of the application to our varied educational interests of that ministerial responsibility which is sound in principle and wise in policy."

If we follow the analogy of representative institutions, Dr. Ryerson's advice was eminently sound, and the action taken by the Parliament of Ontario in placing education under the management of a responsible minister of the Crown defensible. There is no constitutional reason why public opinion should not be brought to bear as directly upon educational questions as upon any other which affect the welfare of the community and the pockets of the taxpayers. Besides, the influence of an officer who is expected to originate as well as to direct legislation is greatly hampered by being prevented from appealing directly to the body which has to pronounce judgment upon the schemes he may formulate as the result of his experience. He may draft bills involving many complicated provisions for the improvement of the schools; he may desire to inaugurate a new policy requiring an extensive knowledge of the school system of other countries, and with consequences and tendencies known only to one who has studied the whole question thoroughly; but if he is not allowed to explain his policy before those having power to accept or reject it, his labour may be of no avail. And so it might happen, as it has happened in the Province of Ontario, that important reforms would be postponed because the only man who could satisfy Parliament with regard to their merits was excluded from the House. To place a bill, no matter how clearly framed by its author, in the hands of a member of Parliament not conversant with the great volume of fact and experience which lies behind it, and who has not made the purpose which it is intended to fulfil a matter of study or a matter of personal concern, usually leads to disaster.

The presence of a Minister of Education on the floor of Parliament has other advantages. As a member of the Executive Government, any legislation he proposes must first have the approval of his colleagues, and to that extent Parliament has an assurance that it has been well considered, for nothing sooner discredits a Government than the introduction of abortive or ill-considered legislation. Moreover, no minister would introduce a bill affecting education or any other great question except upon the conviction that the legislation proposed would be supported by the people. It is not necessary that his bill should be the mere echo of a public opinion clamouring for redress or for advanced legislation. All a minister has to know is that the legislation he proposes, whether called for by a large body of the people or not, will so commend itself to their good judgment that they will take it in trust, partly because of its apparent merits, and partly because of their confidence in the minister or the Government responsible for it. If any explanation is necessary in order to make it clear, that explanation can be given by the minister on the floor of Parliament. True, he is liable to misrepresentation by those who are politically opposed to him. What has been done in good faith may be charged to party exigencies or to political motives, and in that sense public confidence in his educational policy may occasionally be weakened; but this is a form of criticism to which every administrative act of government is exposed.

If office were regarded as a public trust, and the power which it confers upon the holder used for the public good, and that only, theoretically it would be of small consequence how the educational affairs of the country, or indeed any other department of the public service, were administered. But as all legislation is nothing more or less than public opinion crystallized, the more directly that opinion can be brought to bear upon any subject coming within the range of legislation, the more freely and perfectly do representative institutions fulfil their natural and proper function; and if in the fulfilment of that function imperfections are found to prevail, the people, who are the final court of appeal, should be permitted to make their power felt with the fewest obstructions possible.

The Education Department, how composed.—The

Education Department consists of the Executive Government of the province, viz.: the Attorney-General, the Commissioner of Crown Lands, the Provincial Secretary, the Minister of Agriculture, the Provincial Treasurer, the Commissioner of Public Works, the Minister of Education, and any other member of Parliament who may hold a seat in the Government. The Attorney-General, as first minister of the province, acts as chairman. Meetings of the department are held for the transaction of business as may be required. All reports and regulations requiring the consideration of the department are usually submitted by the Minister of Education, and after adoption by the department become operative at once, and are as binding as an act of Parliament. They are subsequently laid before Parliament, and are open to disapproval either in whole or in part.

Jurisdiction of the Department.—The Education Department has jurisdiction over the following classes of schools, viz. :

1. Kindergarten schools for pupils between four and seven years of age, in which instruction shall be given according to kindergarten methods.

2. Public schools for pupils between five and twenty-one years of age, in which instruction shall be given in the elements of an English and commercial education.

3. Night schools for pupils over fourteen years of age, who are unable to attend school during the usual school hours.

4. High schools and collegiate institutes for such pupils as pass the prescribed entrance examination, in which instruction shall be given in the higher branches of a practical English and commercial education, the natural sci-

ences, mathematics, and the Greek, Latin, French, and German languages.

5. Art schools for instruction in mechanical, industrial, and constructive drawing, and other branches of a technical education.

6. County model schools for the training of candidates for teachers' third-class certificates.

7. Normal schools for the training of candidates for teachers' second-class certificates.

8. The normal college for the training of candidates for teachers' first-class certificates, and for the training of teachers of high schools and collegiate institutes.

9. Teachers' institutes for the reading of papers and the general discussion of educational topics.

10. Public libraries, reading-rooms, and evening classes for mechanics and artisans, when aided by the Government.

11. Industrial schools for the instruction in industrial pursuits, with a special view to their moral reformation, of children whose habits render removal from their homes necessary.

12. Separate schools at which the children of Protestants, Roman Catholics, and coloured people respectively may attend, subject to the provisions of the separate schools act hereafter discussed.

Powers of the Education Department.—The Education Department is invested by statute with the power to make regulations—

1. For the classification, organization, government, and examination of the different classes of schools mentioned above, and for the equipment of schoolhouses and the arrangement of school premises.

2. For the authorization of text-books for the use of

pupils, and the selection of books of reference for the use of teachers and public libraries.

3. For determining the qualifications and duties of inspectors, examiners, and teachers.

4. For the payment of the pensions of superannuated inspectors and teachers, and the proper distribution of all moneys set apart by the Legislative Assembly for school purposes.

5. For the study of agriculture, and for scientific instruction as to the nature of alcoholic stimulants and narcotics, with special reference to their effect upon the human system.

Inspectors of high schools, separate schools, county model schools, directors of teachers' institutes, and the masters of normal schools and the practice schools in connection with them, are appointed by the Education Department. Inspectors of public schools are appointed by the Municipal Councils of the county concerned, or by the trustees in the case of cities or towns separated from the county. The department also fixes the fees to be paid by candidates at departmental examinations, and prescribes the forms for school registers and such official reports as boards of trustees and the officers of the department are required to make. All moneys voted by Parliament are paid on the recommendation of the Minister of Education.

Powers of the Minister of Education.—As the executive officer of the Education Department, it is the duty of the Minister of Education to enforce the regulations of the department, and to direct the officers of the department as to the discharge of their duties, and through the official staff of the department to carry on the necessary departmental correspondence. Public-school inspectors, though not appointed by the Minister of Education, are amenable to his authority, and the whole machinery of education subject to his control. He is also *ex officio* a member of the Senate of the Provincial University, and is thus in a position to present the views of the department on educational matters before the Senate, as the governing body of the university. He has power to decide upon all disputes and complaints laid before him, the settlement of which is not otherwise provided for by law, and upon all appeals made to him from the decision of any inspector or other school officer. Should any question arise as to the construction of any statute affecting education, he has the power to submit the matter in dispute to any judge of the High Court for his opinion. The object of this provision of the law is to prevent litigation, and has been found productive of very beneficial results. As a matter of legal procedure, the opinion of the judge is not binding on the parties concerned in the dispute; nevertheless, it is usually accepted. The department is at liberty to pay the costs in such cases, but as the argument is generally conducted through the law officers of the Government, the costs are nominal.

It is the duty of the minister to submit an annual report to Parliament, setting forth the attendance of pupils at the various schools under the jurisdiction of the department, the expenditure of the province for school purposes, the classification of the pupils, and such other information as will enable the members of Parliament to form a correct opinion with regard to the educational progress of the country.

In the event of any legislation being required for the improvement of the school system of the province, the Minister of Education takes charge of such bills as may

ORGANIZATION OF PUBLIC SCHOOLS. 33

be necessary for that purpose, and, except by the defeat of the Government, no legislation can pass which does not meet with his approval. In order to secure greater stability in the organization of the school system of the province, legislation of an important character is submitted to Parliament only at intervals of five years.

Public Schools, how organized.—In considering the organization of the public-school system, the reader must bear in mind—1. That in Ontario, township means a rural district, with a corporation called a Municipal Council. 2. That a county means a number of townships, incorporated towns and villages also under municipal organization, called a County Council. 3. That cities have a municipal organization of their own, and are not under the jurisdiction of the Municipal Council of the county. In some cases towns separate themselves from the municipal jurisdiction of the county, but for present purposes that circumstance need not be considered.

Since the Act of 1871, all public schools are free schools—that is, they are entirely supported by the grant received from the Provincial Government, and by rates levied upon real and personal property. As kindergartens are part of the school system, they too are supported in a similar way—that is, by separate grant from the provincial treasury and by local rates. The trustees may require a fee to be paid by kindergarten pupils for supplies; a fee of twenty cents per month may also be imposed upon public-school pupils for text-books and stationery; but when such fees are imposed, the boards of trustees are required to furnish all text-books and supplies for the use of pupils out of the fees so collected. The limit of the kindergarten age is from four to seven years. The limit of the public-school age is from five to twenty-one. The trustees of rural schools are not, however, obliged by law to provide accommodation for more than two thirds of the number of school children in the section between the ages of five and sixteen years. It has been found from experience that in rural schools the attendance at any time seldom exceeds two thirds of the resident pupils between the ages mentioned.

Public-School Sections.—It is the duty of the Municipal Council of every township to divide the townships into school sections in such a way as to include every part of the township in some section. These sections are numbered 1, 2, 3, 4, etc., and are so known locally, and by the Education Department. To secure the organization of sections of a reasonable size, it is provided that no section shall be formed any portion of which shall be more than three miles in a direct line from the schoolhouse; nor shall any section be formed that contains less than fifty children between the ages of five and twenty-one years, unless such section is more than four square miles in area, except in cases where such area can not be obtained because of lakes or other natural obstacles. In unorganized districts—that is, in districts but sparsely settled, lying toward the north side of the province—school sections are organized by the inspector and the stipendiary magistrate. Where required by public convenience, parts of two or more adjoining townships, or parts of one or more townships and an adjoining town or incorporated village, may be formed into a union section. Such sections are known as union schools, and are in all respects governed as ordinary school sections. If the ratepayers of any township petition any municipal council for the formation of a union school with the adjoining town or incorporated village, the Municipal Councils of the territory concerned are authorized to appoint arbitrators to lay out the Union School Section. If five or more of the ratepayers are dissatisfied with the award of the arbitrators, an appeal lies to the Municipal Council of the county. The Union School Section so formed can not be altered or dissolved for a period of five years. If the territory to be formed into a union school is situated in two adjoining counties, and the Municipal Councils refuse to provide suitable school accommodation, an appeal lies to the Minister of Education, who has authority to appoint arbitrators to consider the matters complained of. There is no appeal from the report of such arbitrators. The school rates in Union School Sections are collected by the tax collectors of the municipality in which each part of the union is respectively situated, and are paid over to the treasurer of the Union School Section. For purposes of inspection a union school is considered to be within the jurisdiction of the inspector in whose territory the schoolhouse of the union section is situated. As it often happens that the assessors of different municipalities adopt a slightly different standard in assessing real and personal property, it is necessary, before rates can be levied fairly on the property of persons residing in a Union School Section, that the assessors of the adjoining municipalities should meet as a Board of Arbitration and adjust in an equitable manner, or, as it is called, equalize, the assessment of a Union School Section. Such an adjustment is required by statute to be made every three years.

Government of Rural Schools.—Rural schools are under the administration of three trustees, who hold office for three years; but, in order to maintain continuity of office, only one retires annually. Any ratepayer, male or female, twenty-one years of age, is eligible to be elected a trustee or to vote at the election of a trustee. As in the case of municipal electors, the franchise presupposes a property qualification, be it ever so small. Supporters of separate schools can not vote for the election of public school trustees, and *vice versa*. The election of school trustees in rural districts is held on the last Wednesday of December, or, if Wednesday be a holiday, then on the next day following, at the hour of ten o'clock in the forenoon. Special meetings may be called by the inspector for filling vacancies. Meetings of ratepayers are organized by the appointment of a chairman and secretary, and the business is conducted in the following order: (*a*) receiving the annual report of the trustees and disposing of the same; (*b*) receiving the annual report of the auditor or auditors and disposing of the same; (*c*) electing an auditor for the ensuing year; (*d*) miscellaneous business; (*e*) electing a trustee or trustees to fill any vacancy or vacancies.

If more persons than one are nominated as school trustee, the majority of the ratepayers present may, by show of hands, declare their choice; or two ratepayers may demand a poll, and in that case the secretary of the meeting shall take down the names of the voters for the different candidates. The poll shall not be kept open later than four o'clock of the afternoon of the day on which the election was commenced, and on the close of the poll the chairman and secretary shall count the votes and declare the person elected who received a majority, or in case of a tie the chairman shall give the casting vote. A trustee elected to fill a vacancy shall hold office only during the unexpired term of the person in whose place he was elected. Any person having served as a trustee may decline to serve for four years next after he retired from office. Any other person chosen as trustee is obliged to serve, or forfeit a penalty of five dollars. Any trustee who accepts and neglects to serve or perform the duties of his office shall be liable to a penalty of twenty dollars, to be recovered before any justice of the peace. Where trustees wilfully neglect or refuse to exercise their corporate powers, or where any moneys are lost to the school section because of their neglect to take proper security, they become personally liable for the loss so incurred. Any trustee who enters into any contract, or who has any pecuniary interest or profit in any contract or agreement in his own name or in the name of another, with the corporation of which he is a member, or any trustee who is convicted of felony or misdemeanour, or who becomes insane, or who absents himself from the meetings of the board without leave, shall, *ipso facto*, vacate his seat. No trustee can hold the office of public-school inspector or teacher within the section of which he is a trustee. Any trustee who knowingly signs a false report of the school section or municipality shall be liable to a penalty of twenty dollars.

In the event of any complaint being made to the inspector with regard to the election of a school trustee, the inspector is authorized to inquire into such complaint, and either to confirm the election or to order a new election. Such complaints must, however, be made within twenty days of the election complained of. The secretary of the school meeting is required by law to transmit to the inspector a copy of the minutes of the annual and all special meetings.

Trustees elected as herein set forth, constitute a corporation and continue in office until their successors are appointed. They are required to use a corporate seal in all transactions of a solemn character; to appoint a secretary or secretary-treasurer, who shall furnish bonds for the proper discharge of the duties of his office. Trustees are required by law to serve without compensation, and the annual meeting at which they are elected to office may, by resolution, order the payment of such a sum as may be agreed upon to the secretary-treasurer for his services as secretary and for attendance to other duties incident to his office. The trustees are required to keep a record of their proceedings, and to produce their books when called for by the auditors or other competent authority. No proceeding of the Board of Trustees is valid unless two at least are present, nor unless notice, either personal or in writing, has been given to every member of the time and place at which a meeting is to be held. The accounts and moneys of the board are audited by two auditors, one appointed by the board and the other by the ratepayers at the annual meeting.

Duties of Trustees.—It is the duty of the Board of Trustees to take charge of the school property, and to dispose, by sale or otherwise, of any school property not required, and to convey the same under their corporate seal. They are to see that the schoolhouse, furniture, outbuildings, and fences are kept in proper repair, and that the well, closets, and premises generally are in a sanitary condition. Should the inspector at any time report any dereliction of duty with regard to these matters, the Minister of Education may withhold the Government grant payable to such section until the orders of the inspector are complied with. They are required to visit the school under their charge, and to see that it is conducted according to the regulations of the Education Department. They are to see that the school is supplied with registers, suitable maps, globes, apparatus, and other equipment. They are at liberty to exempt at their discretion, from the payment of school rates wholly or in part, any indigent persons within the section, and to provide books and other school supplies free to the children of such persons. They are not to allow any unauthorized text-book to be used in their schools, and are to report annually to the ratepayers and to the inspector, on a form provided by the department, the number of pupils in attendance, the time the school was kept open, the receipts and expenditures of the section, the classification of the pupils, etc.

Township Boards.—Where two thirds of the school sections in any township, at the annual meeting of the school sections of the township, agree to abolish boards of trustees, the Municipal Council of the township may pass a by-law for the appointment of township trustees, who shall have the same power with regard to the administration of the schools of the whole township as a board of trustees has with regard to a single school section. Township boards are not received with favour in the province, as only three or four now remain after an experience of over thirty years of the two systems—a board for the township and a board for the section.

School Assessment.—In order to meet the expenses of maintaining the school during the year, the trustees shall submit a statement to the Municipal Council, setting forth the amount of money required for the teacher's salary, the running expenses of the school, and the payment of debentures for the erection of a new schoolhouse, if any, and other proper charges. This amount the Municipal Council levies upon the school section in case of rural schools, or upon the ratepayers in the case of a city, town, or incorporated village, and pays the same to the trustees before the close of the official year. In rural schools, in order to equalize the burdens of taxation, particularly as some school sections are necessarily smaller than others, the Municipal Council is required by law to levy the sum of one hundred dollars for each section upon the assessable property of the whole township. Where a rural school employs an assistant teacher, an additional sum of fifty dollars is levied if the assistant is engaged for the whole year, and proportionately if engaged for six months or over. Out of the provincial treasury there is also paid to each school section, according to the average attendance of pupils, a certain sum of money. The amount paid by the provincial treasury for elementary schools in 1894 was $276,000; the amount raised by taxation on the assessable property was $3,200,000; the amount received from other sources, $1,100,000. These different sums constitute the school revenues of the year, and with these the trustees discharge the financial obligations imposed upon them by law. Should the treasury be depleted at any time, the trustees may issue their promissory notes in order to meet the quarterly payments to be made the teachers on account of salary, but this is the only purpose for which they can bind the corporation by note of hand. Where trustees propose to erect a new schoolhouse, they may levy the whole cost of the schoolhouse upon the section by one rate, and thus pay for it in one payment, or they may take authority from the ratepayers to apply to the Municipal Council for debentures extending over a period of thirty years. The Municipal Council, on such application, is obliged to issue the debentures of the township for this amount. Formerly the debentures were issued by the trustees themselves on the security of the assessment of the section. This mode of issuing debentures was unsatisfactory, as the security was in many cases doubtful, and the interest payable by the trustees proportionately high. The debentures issued by the municipality, being much better security, carry a lower interest. It is to be remembered that, while the whole township is liable for the payment of these debentures, the Municipal Council levies a rate only upon the school section concerned for their payment.

Trustees in Urban Schools.—In every city, town, or incorporated village, the ratepayers are authorized to elect two trustees for each ward into which such city, town, or incorporated village is divided. One trustee in each ward retires annually. Where an incorporated village is not divided into wards, six trustees are elected, two of whom retire annually. Trustees in urban schools are elected at the same time as trustees in rural schools, the proceedings in both cases being identical, except that where the trustees have requested the municipal corporation to provide for their election by ballot, then the election of school trustees is held at the same time and place, and by the same officers as the elections of municipal councillors. The application of the ballot to the election of public-school trustees in urban schools was first permitted in 1886, and has been adopted by about one hundred urban municipalities. In rural districts trustees are elected by open vote only. Complaints with regard to school elections in cities, towns, and incorporated villages are disposed of by the judge of the County Court, and not, as in the case of rural schools, by the inspector.

The trustees of city schools and schools in towns separated from the county have the right to appoint their inspector. They have also the right to employ a superintendent of school buildings and such other officers as may be required for the proper care of school property.

In cities, towns, and incorporated villages, trustees

may furnish the pupils with text-books free of charge, and may impose a rate upon the taxpayers for this purpose. The system of supplying free text-books by a rate upon the property of the citizens has been adopted recently in the city of Toronto. In several other cities textbooks are supplied free, but the expense is met by a monthly fee upon the pupils. The average cost of textbooks, slates, copies, scribblers, etc., in Toronto during the last four years was forty-seven cents per pupil.

Industrial Schools.—Industrial schools were established in 1882 to provide for the education, under proper restraints, of destitute children, or of children who were found wandering without any fixed place of abode, or of children whose parents were not considered competent to exercise proper parental control over their habits. Any person may summon such a child before a police magistrate or a judge of the County Court, and on proof of the child's habits or circumstances the magistrate or judge has authority to commit such child, if under fourteen years of age, to an industrial school, for such time as in the opinion of the magistrate may be necessary for the correction of his habits, but in no case beyond the time when the child would attain the age of sixteen years.

Industrial schools may be established by the public or separate school trustees of any city or town, or by any philanthropic society incorporated for that purpose. Suitable buildings for school purposes, for dormitories, recreation, and industrial pursuits are indispensable. The teaching staff of the school is appointed by the trustees of the public or separate schools, by whom the industrial school was established. The courses of study are the same as those of public schools, and the work of the pupils is subject to the supervision of the public or separate school inspector, as the case may be. Pupils are under the direction of competent instructors in industrial work, and are taught the lighter trades, such as tailoring, shoemaking, printing, and carpentering. In the summer months they are engaged in gardening and on a farm in connection with the school.

Soon after the passing of this act an industrial school was established in the vicinity of Toronto. The cost of providing buildings and classrooms was met partly by a grant from the City Council and partly by contributions from citizens interested in benevolent work. The school is maintained from the following sources: 1. The teaching staff is paid by the Board of Public School Trustees. 2. The Municipal Council of any municipality from which a child is sent to the school pays for its maintenance the sum of two dollars per week. 3. The Provincial Government pays, in addition, ten cents per day for every child committed to the school.

It may be observed that although an industrial school is, for purposes of administration, under the direction of the Board of Trustees or of a society incorporated for that purpose, it is, to all intents and purposes, a provincial school, as a police magistrate or county judge in any part of the province may direct that any child coming within the provisions of the Industrial Schools Act may be sent to whatever school the magistrate or judge may designate.

In 1895 a second industrial school was opened under the direction of the Separate School Board of Trustees for the reception of Roman Catholic children. This also is a provincial school, and subject to the same privileges and conditions as all other industrial schools. There are now in attendance at both schools about two hundred and fifty children.

CHAPTER III.

SCHOOL SITES, PREMISES, AND PUPILS.

It has already been shown that the Municipal Council of every township has authority to divide the township into sections for school purposes. The area of a school section is generally from three to five thousand acres, but this depends to a certain extent upon the assessed value of the land and the density of the population. With the increase of wealth and population the boundaries of the sections are adjusted from time to time by the Council, as the ratepayers may desire, for the convenience and comfort of the school population. So soon as the section is formed, and trustees appointed, a site for a schoolhouse is chosen. This site, however, is subject to the approval of the ratepayers. Should the ratepayers and trustees disagree as to the eligibility or convenience of the site selected, the dispute is referred to three arbitrators—one chosen by the ratepayers, the other by the trustees—the inspector of the school for the district being the third arbitrator. A decision of the majority of the arbitrators binds all parties to the dispute. It sometimes happens that a difference of opinion arises between the owner of the land chosen for a site and the trustees as to the price which should be paid for it. A dispute of this kind is also submitted to arbitrators, who decide as in the former case. If the owner refuses to give a title, then the award of the arbitrators delivered to the trustees may be registered in the proper registry office on the affidavit of the Secretary of the School Board, and such award becomes a legal title for the conveyance of the land. No school site shall be selected in a township within one hundred yards of the garden, orchard, pleasure-ground, or dwelling-house of the owner without his consent. School sites may be enlarged by the trustees without any reference to the ratepayers, but no school site can be changed except with their approval. In cities, towns, or incorporated villages the trustees have power to select school sites without any reference to the ratepayers.

Regulations of the Department respecting Sites.—The regulations of the Education Department provide:

1. Every school site shall be on a well-travelled road, as far removed as possible from a swamp or marsh, and so elevated as to admit of easy drainage.

2. The school grounds shall be properly levelled and drained, planted with shade trees, and enclosed by a substantial fence. Every rural school shall be provided with a woodshed.

3. There shall be a well or other means for procuring water, so placed and guarded as to be perfectly secured against pollution from surface drainage or sewage of every kind.

4. The area of the school site shall be not less than half an acre in extent; and if the school population of the section exceeds seventy-five, the area shall be one acre.

5. The water-closets for the sexes shall be several feet apart, and under different roofs. Their entrances shall be screened from observation. Proper care shall be taken to secure cleanliness, and to prevent unpleasant and unhealthy odours.

6. Suitable walks shall be made from the schoolhouse to the water-closets, so that the closets may be reached with comfort in all kinds of weather.

The first Friday in May is set apart as Arbour day in every rural school for the purpose of planting shade trees, making flower beds, and otherwise improving and beautifying the school grounds. Since the appointment of Arbour day, the inspectors report that over one hundred and fifty thousand shade trees have been planted in the grounds of the schools of the province. Where trustees neglect to keep the school grounds in proper condition, or where they neglect to keep the premises in repair, the Government grant is withheld on the report of the inspector until the regulations of the department are complied with.

Schoolhouses.—The trustees of the school are the sole judges as to the style and material of schoolhouses erected under the Public-School Act. In the early history of the country the log schoolhouse had undisputed possession of the field. It was both primitive in style and very indifferent as to comfort and accommodation. Its place is now occupied by buildings of frame, brick, or stone, all of which have to conform with the regulations of the department. As a rule, trustees before proceeding with the erection of a new schoolhouse receive plans and estimates from a competent architect, and submit them for approval to the county inspector. In the case of large schools, plans are sometimes submitted to the Minister of Education. It is not necessary, in the case of public schools, that the plans should be approved either by the inspector or the department. The trustees are, however, required to provide adequate accommodation in rural districts for at least two thirds of the children between five and sixteen years of age resident in the section, and in urban districts, for all the children between the ages mentioned. Where the average attendance of the section exceeds fifty pupils, the schoolhouse shall contain two rooms; where it exceeds one hundred the schoolhouse shall contain three rooms—an additional room and teacher being required for each unit of fifty pupils in average attendance. In order to prevent overcrowding, it is provided that an area of twelve square feet shall be allowed for each pupil, and at least two hundred and fifty cubic feet of air space. A complete change of air every three hours is the standard rule for ventilation. The heating apparatus must be sufficient to keep a uniform temperature throughout the room of sixty-seven degrees. The light, where possible, must be admitted on the left side of the pupil. Separate entrances with covered porches and suitable cloakrooms are required for the boys and girls.

The teacher is, during the time of his engagement, to a certain extent, the custodian of the school property; he is authorized to make such rules as will insure the keeping of the school grounds and outbuildings in a neat and cleanly condition, and to see that no damage is done to the furniture or other school property. Where repairs are wanted, he is required to give notice in writing to the trustees. He may employ a suitable person to sweep the rooms, dust the walls, seats, desks, and other furniture, where the trustees make no provision for that purpose. The teacher may also complain at any time to the health officer of the district with regard to the unsanitary condition of the schoolhouse or premises.

School Furniture and Equipment.—The regulations of the department with regard to school furniture and equipment are very specific:

1. The seats and desks should be so arranged that the pupils may sit facing the teacher. Not more than two pupils should be allowed to sit at one desk; but single-seated desks are preferable.

2. The heights of the seats should be so graduated that pupils of different sizes may be seated with their feet resting firmly on the floor. The backs should slope backward two or three inches from the perpendicular.

3. The seats and desks should be fastened to the floor in rows, with aisles of suitable width between the rows; passages, at least three feet wide, should be left between the outside rows and the side and the rear walls of the room; and a space, at least five feet wide, between the teacher's platform and the front desks.

4. Each desk should be so placed that its front edge may project slightly over the edge of the seat behind. The desk should be provided with a shelf for pupil's books, and the seat should slope a little toward the back.

5. A sufficient number of seats and desks should be provided for the accommodation of all the pupils ordinarily in attendance at the school. There should be at least two chairs in addition to the teacher's chair.

6. The desks should be of three different sizes. The following dimensions are recommended:

Age of Pupils.	Chairs or Seats.			Desks.			Height next pupil.
	Height.		Slope of back.	Length.		Width.	
	Front.	Rear.		Double.	Single.		
	Inches.	Inches.	Inches.	Inches.	Inches.	Inches.	Inches.
5 to 8 years....	12	11½	2	36	18	12	22
8 to 10 "	13	12¼	2	36	18	12	23
10 to 13 "	14	13½	2½	36	20	13	24
13 to 16 "	16	15½	3	40	22	13	26

SCHOOL SITES, PREMISES, AND PUPILS.

7. There should be one blackboard at least four feet wide, extending across the whole room in rear of the teacher's desk, with its lower edge not more than two and a half feet above the floor or platform; and, when possible, there should be an additional blackboard on each side of the room. At the lower edge of each blackboard there should be a trough five inches wide for holding crayons and brushes, and for collecting the chalk dust, which should be removed every day.*

8. Every school should have at least one globe not less than nine inches in diameter, properly mounted; a map of Canada; a map of Ontario; maps of the world and of the different continents; one or more sets of Tablet Lessons of Part I of the First Reader; a standard dictionary and gazetteer; a numeral frame; a suitable supply of crayons and blackboard brushes; and an eight-day clock.

---

* The following directions for making a blackboard may be found useful:

(*a*) If the walls are brick, the plaster should be laid upon the brick and not upon the laths, as elsewhere; if frame, the part to be used for a blackboard should be lined with boards, and the laths for holding the plaster nailed firmly on the boards.

(*b*) The plaster for the blackboard should be composed largely of plaster of Paris.

(*c*) Before and after having received the first coat of colour it should be thoroughly polished with fine sandpaper.

(*d*) The colouring matter should be laid on with a wide, flat varnish brush.

(*e*) The liquid colouring should be made as follows: Dissolve gum shellac in alcohol, four ounces to the quart; the alcohol should be ninety-five per cent strong; the dissolving process will require at least twelve hours. Fine emery flour, with enough chrome green or lampblack to give colour, should then be added until the mixture has the consistency of thin paint. It may then be applied in long, even strokes, up and down, the liquid being kept constantly stirred.

Duties of Pupils.—In rural districts the schools are open two hundred and eight days. The hours of attendance are from nine o'clock in the forenoon to four o'clock in the afternoon, with a recess of not less than ten minutes both forenoon and afternoon, and at least one hour during midday. Trustees have authority to increase these intervals of recreation. In cities, towns, and incorporated villages the trustees may, by resolution, order the school opened at 9.30 in the forenoon, and closed at 3.30 in the afternoon, with a recess at midday of one hour and a half. In kindergartens pupils are not allowed to attend more than three hours per day. In rural schools every Saturday, Good Friday, Thanksgiving, the Queen's Birthday, Labor day, and every day proclaimed a holiday by municipal or civil authorities are school holidays. The summer vacation begins on the 30th of June and ends on the third Monday of August. The winter vacation begins on the 21st of December and ends on the 2d of January. In cities, towns, and incorporated villages the summer vacation ends on the last Monday of August.

Any child may be refused admission to a public school (except where kindergarten classes are established) before he has attained five years of age. If the schoolroom is not large enough to provide adequately for every pupil between five and sixteen years of age, the trustees may refuse admission to all pupils over sixteen. When the accommodation is ample, pupils may be admitted until they are twenty-one years of age, but no pupil can be counted for the purpose of drawing the Government grant under five (four in the case of kindergartens) or over twenty-one years of age. Every pupil is responsible to his teacher for his conduct to and from school, unless accompanied by his parent or guardian; and the courts have held that a teacher acted within the scope of his authority in punishing pupils for misconduct outside school hours while on their way to or from school. During their attendance at school the pupils are entirely under the teacher's control, and no parent or trustee has a right to interfere with the discipline of the school. The teacher is, however, liable to indictment before a magistrate if he has punished a pupil cruelly or with undue severity. The magistrate is in that case the sole judge of the character of the punishment inflicted, and has authority to impose a reasonable penalty. The punishments which a teacher has a right to inflict are not defined by the regulations of the department. He may prescribe impositions or may detain pupils after school hours, or deprive them of certain privileges as to recreation, or may even inflict corporal punishment. The only rule laid down is that he shall " practise such discipline as would be exercised by a kind, firm, and judicious parent."

Where a pupil is guilty of (*a*) persistent truancy, (*b*) violent opposition to authority, (*c*) the repetition of any offence after being warned, (*d*) habitual and wilful neglect of duty, (*e*) the use of profane or improper language, (*f*) cutting, marring, destroying, or defacing any part of the school property, (*g*) writing any obscene words on the fences, water-closets, or any part of the school premises, (*h*) general bad conduct, injurious to the moral tone of the school, he may be suspended for one month, but immediate notice of such suspension with the reasons therefor shall be given to the parents or guardians and the trustees. In such cases the parents or guardians may appeal against the decision of the teacher to the Board of Trustees, who have the right, on hearing the case, to confirm or set aside the decision of the teacher.

Departmental Regulations.—The regulations with respect to the duties of pupils in public schools are as follows:

1. Every pupil whose name is entered on the register of a public school shall attend punctually and regularly every day of the school term in which his name is entered. Should any pupil absent himself from school except on account of sickness, he shall be liable to such punishment as the teacher may lawfully inflict.

2. No pupil shall be allowed to leave school before the hour for closing except in case of sickness, or at the request, whether oral or written, of his parent or guardian.

3. Any pupil absenting himself from an examination, or from any portion thereof, without permission of the teacher, shall not be admitted to any public school except by the authority of the inspector in writing.

4. Any pupil who is affected with or exposed to any contagious disease shall not be permitted to attend school without a certificate from a physician that there are no sanitary objections to his attendance.

5. Any pupil who shall be adjudged so refractory by the Board of Trustees and by the teacher that his presence in school is injurious to the other pupils, may be expelled, and, without the written consent of the public-school inspector, shall not be allowed to attend any other school in that inspectoral district.

6. Any pupil may be refused admission to a public school who fails to supply himself with the necessary books and stationery required for school purposes, or who fails to pay the fees imposed by the trustees for the current month or quarter, as the case may be, for the free use of books, stationery, and other supplies.

7. Any pupil who injures or destroys school property

may be suspended until the parent or guardian of the pupil makes suitable amends for the property destroyed.

In rural districts the pupils are required to attend the school section in which they reside. Should, however, the schoolhouse in an adjoining section be nearer to their home than the schoolhouse in the section to which they belong, the trustees of such section shall admit them to such school, providing the accommodation of the school is sufficient. When pupils attend any other school than the one in the section in which they reside, they are liable to pay fees equal to the average cost of the instruction of the other pupils of the school. The trustees of the section to which they belong may remit so much of the rates which their parents are obliged to pay in the section to which they belong as would be equal to the fees charged in the neighbouring school, when the distance travelled by the children is three miles or over.

Sanitary Protection.—Should the local Board of Health or any of its officers or members notify the teacher that scarlatina, diphtheria, whooping-cough, measles, or any other contagious disease has broken out in any family, the teacher is authorized to refuse the admission of any member of such family to a public school until satisfactory evidence is received that all danger from such contagious disease has passed away. The trustees of any school may refuse the admission of children who do not produce a certificate of successful vaccination when demanded by the teacher.

In urban schools the trustees may divide the city or town into school districts, and require all pupils to attend the school within the district in which they reside. In schools of two or more stories pupils are required to be trained in fire drill for greater safety in case of fire.

Compulsory Attendance.—The School Act of 1871 provided, for the first time, that every child from the age of seven to twelve years inclusive should have the right to attend some school, or to be otherwise educated, for four months in each year; and any parent or guardian who neglected to carry out this provision of the law was liable to a penalty of five dollars on conviction before a police magistrate or justice of the peace.

In 1891 the provisions of the law with regard to compulsory attendance were made more stringent, and now all children between eight and fourteen years of age are required to attend school for the full term during which the school of the section or municipality in which they reside is open each year, unless excused on the grounds: (a) that the child is under efficient instruction at home or elsewhere; (b) that the child is unable to attend school by reason of sickness or other unavoidable cause; (c) that there is no school within two miles, if such child is under ten years of age, or within three miles, if over that age; (d) that the school accommodation is inadequate, or (e) that the child has been excused for reasons satisfactory to a justice of the peace or to the principal of the school, or (f) that the child has passed the entrance examination prescribed by the education department for admission to a high school. Where any justice of the peace or the principal of the school attended by the child is satisfied that the services of such child are required in husbandry or in urgent household duties, or for the maintenance of such child or some person dependent upon it, the justice of the peace or the principal may relieve such child from attendance at school for a period not exceeding three months in the year. Any person employing a child under fourteen years of age while the school is in session is liable to a penalty of twenty dollars for each offence. The police commissioners, or, where there are no police commissioners, the Municipal Councils of every city, town, or incorporated village are authorized to appoint one or more truant officers for the enforcement of the act. The truant officer is vested with police powers and has authority to enter workshops, factories, stores, and other places where children may be employed, in order to see that the law with regard to school attendance is observed. In rural sections truant officers are appointed by the trustees. A truant officer has power to summon a parent or guardian or any person having legal charge of a child before a magistrate, in case such person neglects the education of any child in his custody. A fine of not less than five nor more than twenty dollars may be imposed in such cases, or the parent or guardian may be placed by the magistrate under bonds in the penal sum of one hundred dollars as a guarantee that he will comply with the law.

Truant officers are required to report annually to the Education Department. The number of truants reported in 1894 was 2,962; the number of complaints made before a magistrate for violation of the act was 135, and the number of convictions 51.

CHAPTER IV.

COURSE OF STUDY IN PUBLIC SCHOOLS.

THE course of study for public schools is divided into five forms. These forms, in graded schools, may be subdivided by the teacher to suit the convenience of the school in the matter of organization and classification. The subjects to be taken up in each form are prescribed by the education department, and no teacher is at liberty to introduce into the form any subject not prescribed, nor to go beyond the limits of work indicated by the department for the form without the concurrence of the inspector and the Board of Trustees. Promotions from one form to another are made by the teacher from time to time, as the attainments of the pupil warrant. The usual practice, however, is to promote pupils before the Christmas and summer holidays. No pupil is allowed to be ranked in one form as to one subject and in another form as to another subject. Should he be deficient in any subject in his form, his promotion is delayed until he is qualified to pass in all the subjects. Should the inspector find at his semi-annual visits to the school that the classification is defective or that the pupils have been promoted to a form which they were not qualified to enter, he is at liberty to readjust the classification as he may deem expedient, and the classification made by the inspector remains in force until the pupils have reached the required standard.

The course of study for public schools covers a period of eleven years, three years of which are usually spent in the first form and two years in each of the other forms. The course includes reading, spelling, writing, arithmetic, grammar, geography, history of England and Canada, drawing, physiology, and temperance. Algebra, geometry, botany, and physics are optional subjects, and are taken in the fifth form, when, in the opinion of the inspector and the trustees, the circumstances of the school will permit of their being taught without injury to the other classes. Physics is not allowed unless a proper supply of apparatus has been provided by the trustees. Agriculture may be taught in any rural school, providing the Board of Trustees, by resolution, require it to be placed upon the course of study.

The limit of a pupil's attainments in each form is partially defined by the regulations and partially by the text-book authorized by the department. This is particularly true of the course in reading, which consists of five readers suitably graduated to the capacity of the pupil in each form. Spelling and language lessons expand according to the age and attainments of the pupils. In writing, blackboard exercises are used in the first form. In the second form both writing and drawing are systematically taught in a graduated series of copy books and drawing books, which are numbered like the readers. Geography, grammar, and composition are also taught orally in the first and second forms; in subsequent forms a text-book is used. History, except incidentally, as suggested by the reading lessons, is not taken up by the aid of a text-book until the fourth form. Physiology and temperance are taught in the first three forms conversationally, and by the aid of a text-book in the fourth form. Pupils in the first form are expected to be able to read and write numbers up to one thousand, and to be expert in all ordinary calculations in addition and subtraction. In the second form they are expected to read and write numbers up to one million, with the addition of multiplication and division. Problems involving business transactions of a familiar kind and simple exercises in mental arithmetic are also required in both forms. In the third form the exercises in arithmetic consist of bills and accounts, elementary reduction, and the compound rules; in the fourth form, of multiples, fractions, percentage, and interest; in the fifth form, more difficult exercises in the subjects of the fourth form and the mensuration of surfaces.

Within the limitations mentioned there will necessarily be a great variety of standards. To define a course, which theoretically should determine the attainments of pupils of a given age and within a given range, is comparatively an easy matter; but whether the work within these limitations will be of a high educational value depends entirely upon the teacher. The department has, however, in its instructions to teachers and inspectors suggested certain lines of work in every subject for the direction of the teacher, rather as warnings against bad teaching than as arbitrary standards of excellence. The following outline indicates the scope of each subject in the public-school course :

Reading.—The teacher shall adopt the phonic method. Great care should be taken in analyzing the sounds of which every word is composed. A new word should, where possible, be first introduced to a child's notice through the real object which it represents. In teaching the word "hat," the object "hat" should be before the child. Where the object is not available, a picture of the object should be drawn upon the board and underneath the name of the object written. When the phonic sounds of one word are mastered, other words with similar phonics should be practised upon—such as hat, bat, rat. Strict attention should be paid to articulation and enunciation, and all consonant sounds should be clearly vocalized. Final letters should never be obscured. Small sentences should be formed with every word as soon as learned, that pupils might understand its relation to other words in sentence-building. Pupils should be taught to read with clearness and fluency, the standard of expression both as to inflection and emphasis being that of ordinary conversation. Every new word in the lesson should be fully explained by the teacher, and pupils should be taught to form small sentences orally, using a new word in its proper sense and properly related to other words in the sentence. Every reading lesson should be made both a language lesson and a lesson in literature. Reading should be fluent, natural, and agreeable. Fluency can only be obtained when the pupil has been so thoroughly drilled in word forms as to be able to recognise every word the moment his eye rests upon it. Where this is not done there will be hesitation and a strong tendency to monotonous reading. Pupils should be frequently called upon to read easy lessons which they have thoroughly mastered in order to train the voice to respond quickly to what the eye observes. Pupils should not be interrupted in their reading to correct errors. Natural reading is the expression of the written characters of the book as the same ideas would be expressed in conversation. There can be no natural reading unless the pupil comprehends the thought to be expressed. Before a sentence, therefore, is made the subject of a reading exercise, the teacher should see that the pupil comprehends its meaning. A reading lesson to be agreeable should be correct as to pitch, emphasis, and accent. To secure excellence in this particular the teacher should recall the instruction received in the training school. Where pupils are deficient in the articulation of any particular sound, constant drill should be given in the words containing this sound.

Spelling.—Spelling should be taught from dictation first and orally afterward. The pupil should be able to spell and write legibly every word in the reading book. In addition to the words of the text-book, the pupils should be asked to spell the names of objects in the schoolroom. To excite interest in spelling, they might be asked to make lists of all the animals they have seen, or of all the trees they could name, or of all their classmates, or of the different articles of food they use, and so on. In this way spelling would bear a more vital relation to their daily life, and its usefulness would be more apparent.

Writing.—Writing should begin with reading. The small letters should be taught first. The pupil should be required to maintain a proper position at his desk, to hold his pen or pencil after some approved form, and to obtain as early as possible the necessary freedom of wrist and arm. No careless exercise in writing should pass without criticism. Copy books should be neatly kept; undue haste in writing should be restrained; legibility and neatness should characterize every exercise. Careful attention should be paid to the connection and spacing of letters. For correcting errors the blackboard should be freely used, and the attention of the pupil frequently directed to the headlines in the authorized copy books.

Language Lessons.—Language lessons, as here defined, include grammar and composition. In the lower forms these exercises are mainly oral. Pupils should be taught to speak with reasonable fluency. It might be necessary sometimes to restrain rather than to stimulate quickness of utterance. Statements should, except where it would appear pedantic, be complete sentences correct as to syntax and the use of the different parts of speech. New words that occur in the reading lessons should be used for sentence-building, and pupils should be trained to write summaries of their lesson in their own language. At latest, in the second form, they should be required to give an account of some visit they have paid to a friend, or to describe some object which came under their observation. It may be desirable in some cases, by way of suggesting ideas, to tell them a short story and ask them to reproduce it. Every exercise of this kind should be carefully criticised by the teacher as to arrangement, punctuation, penmanship, the use of capital letters, etc. As the pupil advances these exercises may be made more difficult. The parts of speech should be taught inductively—that is, from the place they serve in language. Formal grammar from a text-book might be used to supplement the oral lessons; similarly with errors in conversation. The teacher's aim should be to encourage the use of good English, to discredit the use of expressions not sanctioned by standard writers, and to cultivate accuracy, conciseness, and clearness of expression.

Geography.—The object of geography is to learn the position of different parts of the earth in relation to each other. These positions, generally speaking, exist under four relations—north, south, east, and west. The first lessons in geography should be to teach the child these relations, and the schoolhouse should be to him the central point of his observation. All objects in the schoolroom and within the range of his vision outside of the schoolroom should be taught from this standpoint. Similarly, the geographical terms to be learned first are those applicable to his own locality, whatever they may be, such as hill, valley, creek, or river; if inland, the terms should be varied so that geography in its first stage may be an object lesson. Other geographical terms might be learned by artificially producing the objects themselves in the school ground or on a sand board. Natural phenomena, such as clouds, rains, snow, winds, etc., should also form the subject of lessons under this heading. In this way a preparation for map geography should be made in the first form. The pupil might then be introduced to a map of the world, and, having become familiar with land and water, would soon comprehend the relation of the continents and great oceans to each other. The animals and plants of each country, the occupations of the people, the adaptability of their occupations to the climate and the products of the country, the direction of the water course and why, the location of cities and why, the phenomena of earthquakes and trade winds and ocean currents should be considered. The course prescribed in the public-school geography should be completed at the end of the fourth form, but no text-book should be introduced until after the pupils have passed through the second form. The text-book in advanced geography should be used in the fifth form.

History.—History should be taught incidentally with the reading lessons in the second form, and conversationally. The subject should be presented in such a way as to excite the interest of pupils to further inquiry for themselves, and as a narrative of the habits, occupations, amusements, and modes of living of the people described, rather than as an account of their forms of government and political institutions. The names of some distinguished men of whom the pupils may have heard or read might be taken as a centre around which the events of their time clustered, or the achievements of such men in defending their country or improving its social condition, or anecdotes illustrating great events in history, and the courage and self-denial of men who had served the country at their peril might be told, and the patriotic efforts of the noted men and women of the past cited to stir up a similar spirit in the minds of the pupils. Special attention should be paid to the history of Canada—how it is governed, its relations to the empire, and the obligations which citizenship imposes upon every Canadian to advance its prosperity. The authorized text-book in history* should be introduced in the fourth form.

Drawing.—Drawing should be taught in the first form from the blackboard. In the other four forms it should be taught by a series of graduated exercise books and models.

Physiology and Temperance.—This subject, as far as

---

* The Public-School History compresses in two hundred pages the principal events of English and Canadian history from the earliest time down to the present day. It is intended as a guide to the teacher with respect to the events which should engage his attention. He is therefore expected to draw upon his wider knowledge of the subject and his general reading for such material as may be necessary to stimulate the interest of his pupils. A text-book in history adapted to the psychological conditions of the pupil at his age would be too large and too expensive for convenient use in a public school. In the fifth form a larger text-book is required in which the subject of English and Canadian history is treated in greater detail.

the end of the third form, should be taught by familiar conversations with the pupils, and by the use of illustrated charts and blackboard drawings. The object of this course should be to make the pupils acquainted with the different organs of the human body, and the best means of preserving the healthy action of these organs. The dangerous effects of stimulants and narcotics should be impressed upon the pupil by showing how they destroy the healthy action of the nervous system and the stomach. The moral danger consequent upon dissipation should also be pointed out. The text-book in this subject is so suggestive as to render definite instructions to the teacher unnecessary.

Literature.—The object of the study of literature is to enable the pupil to apprehend clearly the meaning of such reading matter as may be placed in his hands. To this end, he should be taught to substitute for words or phrases in the book, words of his own, without impairing the sense of the passage; to illustrate and show the appropriateness of important words or phrases; to distinguish between synonyms in common use; to paraphrase difficult passages so as to show the meaning clearly; to show the connections of the thoughts of any selected passage; to explain allusions; to write explanatory or descriptive notes on proper or other names; to show that he has studied the lessons thoughtfully, by being able to give an intelligent opinion on any subject treated of therein that comes within the range of his experience or comprehension; and especially to show that he has entered into the spirit of the passage by being able to read it with proper expression. He should be required to memorize passages of special beauty from the selections prescribed, and to reproduce in his own words the substance of any of these selections or of any part thereof. He should also obtain some knowledge of the authors from whose works these selections have been made.

Music.—Kindergarten songs should be taught in the first form; in the other forms rote singing and musical notation. Staff notation or the Tonic Sol Fa system may be used at the option of the teacher.

Drill and Calisthenics.—The different extension movements prescribed in the authorized text-book on the subject should be frequently practised, not only during recess but during school hours. In addition, the boys should be formed into companies and taught the usual squad and company drill, and the girls should be exercised in calisthenics. Accuracy and promptness should characterize every movement.

Moral and Religious Instruction.—No course of moral instruction is prescribed. The teacher should, however, by his personal example and by instruction as well as by the exercise of his authority, imbue every pupil with respect for those moral obligations which underlie a well-formed character. Respect for those in authority and for the aged, courtesy, manliness, reverence, temperance, truthfulness, honesty, etc., can best be inculcated as the occasion arises for referring to them. The religious exercises of the school should be conducted without haste and with the utmost reverence and decorum. Trustees and teachers will be guided as to the nature and extent of religious instruction by the regulations on this subject.

Reviews and Recitations.—Every Friday forenoon should be devoted to a review of the week's work, and the afternoon to exercises tending to relieve the usual routine of the schoolroom, while promoting the mental and moral culture of the pupils. The teacher should encourage the pupils to prepare dialogues, readings, recitations, and songs for the Friday afternoon school sessions. He should also choose some topic for a familiar lecture or for discussion, or read some literary selections, making such comments as are likely to promote a love of reading, and quicken the interest of the scholars in the work of the school. Familiar illustrations in elementary science should be given. The girls should receive suitable instruction in plain sewing.

Optional Subjects.—The course of study in the first four forms is obligatory. No pupil can be excused from the study of any subject prescribed for his form. In the fifth form, as already stated, algebra, physics, and botany are optional, and may be omitted, or one or more taken up as may be deemed expedient by the inspector and the trustees. Physics must be taught experimentally and with suitable apparatus. Botany must be taught from the actual plants, and teachers are recommended to take their pupils into the fields for the purpose of observing the habits of plants, and for collecting their own specimens. The following is the outline of the course in the optional subjects prescribed by the Education Department:

Algebra: Elementary rules; factoring; greatest common measure; least common multiple; simple equations of one unknown quantity; simple problems.

Physics: An experimental course defined as follows: (*a*) Properties of matter: Sensations and things; causes and effects; absence of chance in the order of Nature; matter; the molecule; constitution of matter; physical and chemical changes; inertia; force; energy; phenomena of attraction; cohesion; compressibility; elasticity, etc. (*b*) Sound: Vibrations and waves; production and propagation of sound waves; velocity; reflection; echoes; refraction; intensity; pitch; difference between noise and music. (c) Light: Propagation; reflection; images formed by plane and spherical mirrors; refraction; lenses; dispersion; selective absorption; colour. (d) Electricity: Voltaic cells; polarization; heating, luminous, chemical, and magnetic effects, produced by the electric current; the electric bell, the telegraph, the telephone, the electric light; magnetism.

Botany: The practical study of representatives of the following natural orders of flowering plants: Ranunculaceæ, Cruciferæ, Malvaceæ, Leguminosæ, Rosaceæ, Sapindaceæ, Umbelliferæ, Compositæ, Labiatæ, Cupuliferæ, Araceæ, Liliaceæ, Iridaceæ, Coniferæ, and Gramineæ. A knowledge of structure obtained with the use of the microscope. Attention to drawing and description of plants supplied, and to the classification of these. Comparison of different organs, morphology of root, stem, leaves, and hairs, parts of the flowers, reproduction of flowering plants, pollination, fertilization, and the nature of fruits and seeds.

Dual Languages.—Although the population of the province of Ontario is chiefly composed of English-speaking people, there are certain settlements in which the French and German languages prevail to such an extent that many children of school age are unable to speak the English language when first admitted to school. The national preferences of their parents naturally lead them, in such cases, to prefer teachers who can speak their own language. The effect of this was that children of French and German parentage often grew up without an adequate knowledge of English, either spoken or written. To prevent the disadvantages in an English-speaking province arising from this condition of things, the Education Department provided a series of readers so prepared that the pupil, whose native language was French or German, would find the lesson for the day in the French or German language on one page and the same lesson in English on the opposite page and by this means his native language was made to assist him in acquiring a language of which he had no knowledge. These readers are called French-English or German-English, according as they are adapted to the French or the German language, and their use has produced very satisfactory results.

In order, however, that the teachers whose native language was French or German, and many of whom were unable to pass the examination required of the ordinary teacher, might be fitted professionally for their duties, the Education Department established two training schools in the French counties on the principle of the county model school. These schools are under a competent principal, familiar with both languages. The course of study is the same as that required for other teachers, but the standard of examination is not quite so high. The examination of the candidates is conducted in English, but an additional paper is required in French composition and grammar. These schools receive special aid from the provincial treasury.

As there was a tendency in some parts of the province, particularly in French settlements, to ignore the use of English in the public schools, the Education Department by regulation prescribed that every exercise and recitation from the English text-books, used in public schools, should be conducted in the English language. Recitations in French or German might, however, be taken in the language of the text-book. It was also provided that all communication between teacher and pupil in regard to matters of discipline, and in the management of the school, should be in English, except so far as this is impracticable, by reason of the pupil not understanding English. The dual language text-books are to be used only where the pupil's knowledge of English is insufficient for the use of the English text-book. Where the parents or guardians require the French or German language to be taught to their children, the trustees, with the concurrence of the inspector, are authorized to see that instruction is given in reading, grammar, and composition in the language of such parents or guardians.

CHAPTER V.

TEACHERS AND THEIR QUALIFICATIONS.

TEACHERS of public schools are divided into three classes, according to their literary and professional attainments. Those who obtain the highest rank awarded by the department are called first-class teachers, and the others second- and third-class teachers respectively.

Before any person can be admitted to the teaching profession he must be a subject of her Majesty, and at least eighteen years of age; he must also furnish satisfactory proof of good moral character; and have passed the examinations prescribed by the Education Department.

The regulations respecting the qualifications, courses of study, and examinations of male and female teachers are identical. Certificates of the first and second class are valid during good behaviour; certificates of the third class are valid for a period of three years only; but every certificate, whether of the first, second, or third class, is valid in the whole province. In certain counties where the settlements are sparse, and the facilities for training teachers somewhat limited, certificates may be granted by a local Board of Examiners for a period of from one to three years, valid in the district only. Temporary certificates, in the case of an emergency, such as sickness, or where there is a scarcity of teachers, may be given by the inspector until the next departmental examination. Similarly, the term of a third-class certificate may be extended beyond the three years for which it is ordinarily valid, but no such extension shall be granted unless it is shown that the trustees have exercised due diligence, by advertisement or otherwise, to obtain a qualified teacher. The object of this regulation is to protect teachers possessing the energy to qualify themselves as required by the department from being displaced by adventurers of inferior qualifications. The consent of the Minister of Education is necessary for the issue of temporary or extended certificates.

The certificate of any teacher guilty of immorality, or found by the inspector to be incapable or inefficient, or who knowingly violates the School Act or the regulations of the Education Department, may be suspended by the inspector. Notice of such suspension shall be given in writing to the trustees concerned, and to the teacher, with a statement of the reason for such suspension. The Board of Examiners for the district, of which the inspector is a member, are by statute authorized to consider all cases of suspension, and to decide as to the merits of each case. If the suspension is confirmed, the teacher's agreement with his trustees is vacated, and he is disqualified for engaging in another school until the suspension is removed. A teacher who enters into an agreement with a Board of Trustees, and wilfully neglects to carry out his agreement, is liable to the suspension of his certificate by the inspector under whose jurisdiction he may be for the time being.

Qualifications of Teachers.—There is no special provision for the literary training of public-school teachers in the province of Ontario. The course of study prescribed in public and high schools is delimited in different forms in such a manner that candidates for teachers' certificates may, by taking the course of a particular form, pass the examinations which qualify them for whatever grade of certificate they desire. For instance, the course of study in the fifth form of the public school, or the second form of the high school, qualifies for the literary basis of a third-class certificate, and the courses in the third and fourth forms of the high school qualify for the literary basis of a second- and a first-class certificate respectively. It must be remembered, however, that the nonprofessional work for a teacher's certificate is, by the regulations of the Education Department, entirely distinct from the professional course of training, without which there is no admission to the teaching profession at any stage. The object of the department is to use the machinery of the public and high schools for the education of teachers as well as for the general education of the people. The nonprofessional work, which is done in normal schools in the United States and Great Britain, is done partially by the public schools, but mainly by the high schools and collegiate institutes in Ontario. In this way the duplication of courses is avoided, and the public treasury is relieved of what would be a very heavy charge, if the attempt was made to establish a sufficient number of normal schools to keep up the needful supply of teachers. So long as the department controls, as it does control, the examinations by which the literary attainments of the pupils at high schools and collegiate institutes are tested, it is considered as of little consequence by whom their teachers are appointed or paid. Indeed, so far has this principle been ingrafted upon the system that undergraduates in the university, at certain stages of their university course, are regarded as having attained to the literary standards required by the department without any other examination than that passed by the university authorities.

What the department wants in the teacher is accuracy of knowledge and breadth of culture. If the standards of the university satisfy these requirements, as they invariably do, there is no loss but rather substantial gain to the public in recognising such standards as the literary basis for teachers in public schools. The regulations therefore provide that the standing of the second, third, or fourth year in arts after a regular course in any chartered university in the British dominions shall be accepted in the Education Department in lieu of the literary standing required for third-, second-, and first-class teachers respectively.

Subjects of Third-Class Standing.—Candidates for the literary standing required of third-class teachers are examined in the following subjects—viz., reading, writing, drawing, bookkeeping, English grammar and rhetoric, English composition, English literature, history of Great Britain and Canada, geography, botany and physics, arithmetic and mensuration, algebra and geometry.

In reading and writing no arbitrary standard can be fixed, the degree of excellence depending entirely upon the judgment and appreciation of the examiner.

In English grammar and rhetoric candidates are examined as to etymology and syntax, including the inflection, classification, and elementary analysis of words, and the logical and rhetorical structure of the sentence and paragraph, with exercises chiefly on passages from authors not prescribed in the course of study.

In English poetical literature candidates are expected to possess an intelligent and appreciative comprehension of the prescribed texts, and to memorize the finest passages of poetry which these texts contain. The texts selected for special study are taken from the reader used in the form, and include selections from the best English and American poets. These texts are changed every year, for the purpose of widening the acquaintance of the candidates with the best literature of the day.

In composition the examination consists of an essay on some familiar subject. In order to pass in composition, legible writing, correct spelling and punctuation, and the proper construction of sentences are indispensable. The candidate is also required to give attention to the structure of the essay, to the effective ordering of the thought, and to the accurate employment of a good English vocabulary. The essay is not to exceed three pages of foolscap in length, while quality, not quantity, is the main consideration.

In history the examination consists of a general knowledge of the outlines of Canadian and British history.

In geography the candidate is expected to have studied the physical features of the earth, its natural products and inhabitants, the occupations of the people, and the relations of physical conditions to the animal and vegetable world; transcontinental commercial highways, and their relations to centres of population; internal commercial highways of Canada, and the chief internal commercial highways of the United States; the commercial relations of Great Britain and her colonies; forms of government in the countries of the world, and their relation to civilization; a general knowledge of mathematical geography, such as the form, size, and motions of the earth; its relations to the sun, light, temperature, etc.

In botany the students are examined with regard to

the different orders of flowering plants usually found in the locality—the orders on which they are examined being set forth in detail in their course of study. The examination consists of a drawing and description of the plants submitted by the examiner, and a comparison of their different organs, such as root, stem, leaves, and flowers, including fertilization and the nature of fruits and seeds.

In physics the course of study covers such subjects as the phenomena of gravitation, the laws of attraction, specific gravity; the meaning of force, work, energy; properties and laws of gases, liquids and solids, and the elementary laws of heat.

In arithmetic and mensuration the examination is limited to fractions, commercial arithmetic and mensuration of rectilinear figures—the circle, sphere, cylinder, and cone.

In algebra the examination is limited to the elementary rules, highest common measure, lowest common multiple, equations of one, two, and three unknown quantities and simple problems, and in geometry the first book of Euclid with easy deductions.

Subjects of Second-Class Standing.—Candidates for second-class standing are examined in the same subjects as those prescribed for third-class standing. The papers in geography and English are more comprehensive, and consequently more difficult.

To the English and Canadian history required for third-class standing are added outlines of Roman history to the death of Augustus, and of Greek history to the battle of Chæronea.

To the algebra are added square root, indices, surds, quadratics of one and two unknown quantities; and to Euclid, Books II and III.

Candidates for second-class standing are also required to take Latin and Greek and one modern language, or Latin and two modern languages and chemistry, or Latin and one modern language and a full science course. Putting the course for second-class standing more simply, every candidate must take Latin and French and Greek, or, if he prefer, he may take Latin, German, and Greek; or Latin, French, German, and chemistry; or Latin, French, physics, chemistry, and botany; or Latin, German, physics, chemistry, and botany. The theory of the course is that Latin is the basis of a good English education; but, in order to secure flexibility and breadth of culture, the candidate may follow his preference for language or for science, according to the limitations above mentioned.

The examination in classics consists of translation from and into English of passages from the prescribed texts, translation at sight, and questions in grammar from the prescribed texts.

Subjects of First-Class Standing.—Candidates who write on the subjects required for first-class standing are assumed to have already passed the examination required for second-class standing, with the exception of English composition, English literature, algebra, and geometry. When they enter upon the preparation of the work required for first-class standing, they are free to give their whole attention to the courses of study required for this examination.

In English literature the texts are similar to those prescribed for matriculation into the university, and consist of complete poems from the best English and American writers; for instance, The Ancient Mariner, from Coleridge; Evangeline, from Longfellow; The Merchant of

Venice and Richard II, from Shakespeare; several poems and sonnets from Wordsworth, and a few selections from Campbell. The selections named do not include all that are required to be studied, but are simply given by way of illustration.

To the algebra required for second-class standing are added the theory of divisors, ratio, proportion and variation, progression, notation, permutation and combinations, binominal theorem, interest forms and annuities.

To geometry are added the fourth and sixth books of Euclid, and the definitions of Book V, and a short course in trigonometry. Biology is added to the science course. The classical and modern language courses are proportionately more difficult.

Specialists' Certificates.—In view of the desire for pre-eminence in the higher departments of education, provision is made for those who desire to give special attention to some department of study. The Education Department makes no provision for examinations of this kind, but accepts the honours which candidates may obtain at a university as evidence of their required qualification. Specialist certificates are awarded, therefore, to any person obtaining honours at a university in the province of Ontario in English and history, or in mathematics, or in classics, or in French and German, or in science. As the courses in the different universities vary somewhat, the Education Department, in order to secure uniformity in its standards, requires a candidate for a specialist certificate to submit to the department the papers on which he wrote, a confidential statement from the registrar of the university of the marks obtained on each paper, and such other marks as may have been awarded at any oral or practical examination in the subjects of his course. The department reserves to itself the right to adjust the results to the departmental standard adopted for a specialist certificate.

A specialist certificate is also given to those who take an extended course in bookkeeping, covering such subjects as single and double entry, warehousing, steamboating, municipal bookkeeping, commission business, joint-stock companies, etc.; commercial arithmetic, including interest, sinking funds, annuity tables, stocks, exchange, etc.; banking, including the business of banks in all its variations, and the laws of business as applied to contracts, chattel mortgages, corporations, telegraphs, patents, etc.; stenography and business correspondence.

Preparation of Examination Papers.—The literary examinations of candidates for the three grades of certificates already referred to are based upon examination papers prepared under the direction of the Education Department. By arrangement with the Senate of the Provincial University, a Board of Examiners is constituted for the whole province, four being appointed by the Senate and four by the Department of Education. This board is called a Joint Board of Examiners. Their duties are twofold : first, to select suitable persons to prepare examination papers; and, secondly, to appoint suitable persons to read the answers of the candidates. As the literary standing of first- and second-class teachers corresponds with the qualifications required for senior and junior matriculations respectively, the university is, by this arrangement with the department, enabled to dispense with its own matriculation examination. Through its representatives on the joint board it has all the control necessary to maintain its own literary standards. The cost of an extra examination is also saved, as well as the time of candidates who might desire the twofold advantage of matriculation and the literary standing of a teacher. Experience has shown that many who qualify themselves to teach a public school, finding that the same qualification admits them to the university, are led afterward to take a university course.

In constituting the Committee of Examiners for preparing papers, the joint board is instructed to select such committee from persons qualified by experience as teachers either in a university or high school. The idea underlying this instruction is that persons who have taught a subject are the best qualified to prepare suitable tests for those who are to be examined upon it. A similar limitation is imposed upon the joint board in selecting a committee to read the examination papers, with this additional restriction, that such committee must be selected from persons who hold a degree in arts from some university in the British dominions, and who are actually engaged in teaching. The theory of this instruction is that the person engaged in teaching a subject is familiar with the most modern and most approved methods of dealing with it. His knowledge of the subject itself is also likely to be more accurate, and justice is therefore more likely to be done to the candidate. The committee charged with the preparation of the examination papers consists of at least one person specially skilled in the subject. If not an honour man of his university, he must have been a teacher of recognised merit in his department.

The procedure in preparing examination papers is briefly as follows:

The joint board, at a meeting usually held six months before the date of the examination, meets and selects from among the professors and lecturers of the different universities of the province, and such other persons as acquired distinction as high-school teachers, the requisite number of persons to constitute a committee for the preparation of examination papers. Within a month or six weeks thereafter, each member of the committee appointed to prepare a paper transmits a manuscript copy thereof confidentially to the Minister of Education. This manuscript is placed in the hands of a confidential printer employed by the department, whose office is in the departmental buildings. When the different papers are in type, proofs are sent to the various members of the committee for consideration. A meeting of the committee is then called, and each paper is submitted to the judgment of the whole committee. Although the responsibility of preparing a suitable paper primarily rests on the member of the committee appointed for that purpose, yet, by the rules of the joint board, approved by the department, the whole committee is held responsible for every paper finally passed. The papers, having been approved by the committee, are initialled by the chairman and then returned to the confidential printer, and are ready to be struck off. While the joint board is responsible for the *personnel* of the committee, it has no responsibility with regard to the character of the examination papers. This rests entirely on the persons appointed for that purpose; and, in order to increase the sense of that responsibility, the name of the person or persons who prepared the paper appears on the face of it.

Mode of Conducting the Examinations.—Candidates who propose to write for matriculation into the university or for a teacher's certificate of any grade are required to notify the public-school inspector of the district in which they reside, not later than the 24th day of May immediately preceding. As a matter of public convenience this examination is held at the beginning of the summer holidays. Every high school and collegiate institute is an examination centre, but examinations may be held, with the approval of the department, at other places. In notifying the inspector of their intention to come up for examination, the candidates intimate the class of certificate for which they propose to write, and the optional subjects, if any, which they desire to take, at the same time transmitting to the inspector an examination fee of five dollars, if it is proposed to take a full examination, or a smaller fee for a partial examination. When the time for receiving notices expires, the inspector makes a list of the applicants on the form prescribed and transmits the same, with the fees, to the Minister of Education. These lists are entered in the office of the registrar of the department, and a number is assigned to each candidate. The public-school inspector for the district presides at the examination, but where, from the number of candidates, more rooms than one are required, additional presiding examiners may be appointed with the approval of the Education Department, preference being given for this duty to members of the teaching profession.

Where the inspector does not consider himself competent to select the plants for the examination in botany, the Minister of Education appoints some suitable person for this purpose. The specimens for the examination in zoölogy are sent directly to the presiding examiner from the Education Department.

When the candidates for examination assemble, places are allotted to them at least five feet apart, and all charts or maps having reference to the subjects of examination are removed from the room. A diagram of the room showing the position occupied by each candidate during the examination is transmitted to the department with the examination papers, in order to facilitate the detection of candidates who may be suspected of copying.

During the examination no person except the presiding examiner is allowed to be present in the room in which the candidates are writing. The candidates are furnished by the presiding examiner with the necessary stationery and writing supplies, and with envelopes in which they are to place their answer papers at the close of the examination in each subject. The presiding examiner is directed as to the time to be allowed for each subject by a time table prepared by the Education Department.

Duties of Candidates.—Before distributing the examination papers the presiding examiner reads the instructions of the department with respect to the duties of candidates, which are as follows:

1. Each candidate shall satisfy the presiding examiner as to his personal identity before the commencement of the second day's examination, and any person detected in attempting to personate a candidate shall be reported to the department.

2. Candidates shall be in their allotted places before the hour appointed for the commencement of the examination. If a candidate be not present till after the appointed time, he shall not be allowed any additional time. No candidate shall be permitted, on any pretence whatever, to enter the room after the expiration of an hour from the commencement of the examination.

3. No candidate shall leave the room within *one hour* after the distribution of the examination papers in any subject; and if he leave, then he shall not be permitted to return during the examination on such subject.

TEACHERS AND THEIR QUALIFICATIONS. 83

4. Every candidate shall conduct himself in strict accordance with the regulations. Should he give or receive any aid or extraneous assistance of any kind, in answering the examination questions, or if he leaves his answers exposed so that any candidate may copy from him, he will forfeit any certificate he may have obtained. Should such candidate have failed at the examination, he shall be debarred for two years from writing at any departmental examination.

5. Every candidate shall write the subject of examination very distinctly at the top of each page of his answer papers, in the middle. If a candidate writes his name or initials, or any distinguishing sign or mark on his answer papers by which his identity may be disclosed, they will be cancelled.

6. Candidates, in preparing their answers, shall write on one side only of each sheet, and shall mark the sheets in each subject in the order of the questions, as 1st, 2d, 3d, etc.; and on the last sheet shall write distinctly the total number of sheets inclosed in the envelope, fold them once across, place them in the envelope provided by the department, write on the outside of the envelope the subject of examination only, and on the slip provided, his name in full (surname preceding), and then securely fasten the slip to the envelope, as instructed by the presiding examiner.

Duties of Presiding Examiners.—Having read the instructions, the presiding examiner is himself directed to proceed as follows:

1. Punctually at the time appointed for the commencement of each examination the presiding examiner shall, in the examination room and in the presence of the candidates and other examiners (if any), break the seal of the

envelope containing the examination papers, and give them to the other examiners and the candidates. The papers of only one subject shall be opened at one time.

2. Should any candidate be detected in talking or whispering, or in copying from another, or allowing another to copy from him, or in having in his possession, when in the room, any book, notes, or anything from which he might derive assistance in the examination, it shall be the duty of the examiner, if he obtain clear evidence of the fact at the time of its occurrence, to cause such candidate at once to leave the room; nor shall such candidate be permitted to enter during the remaining part of the examination, and his name shall be struck off the list. If, however, the evidence be not clear at the time, or be obtained after the conclusion of the examination, the examiner shall report the case to the department.

3. Punctually at the expiration of the time allowed the examiner shall direct the candidates to stop writing, and cause them to hand in their answer papers immediately, duly fastened in the envelopes.

4. The examiner shall keep upon his desk the certified list of the candidates, and as each paper in any subject is handed in, he shall check the same by entering the figure " 1 " opposite the name of the candidate, on the form provided. After the papers are handed in, the examiner shall not allow any alterations to be made in them, and he shall be responsible for their safe keeping until transmitted to the Education Department, or placed in the hands of the presiding examiner.

5. The presiding examiner, at the close of the examination on the last day, shall secure in a separate parcel the fastened envelopes of each candidate, and on the same day shall forward by express (prepaid), or deliver to the

Education Department the package containing all the parcels thus separately secured. The papers are to be arranged in the alphabetical order of the surnames of the candidates. The inspector or presiding examiner shall at the same time sign and forward a solemn declaration to the Minister of Education in the following terms:

(1) I, the undersigned, hereby solemnly declare that I read the regulations to the candidates fifteen minutes before the time at which the examination papers were to be submitted, as per time table.

(2) That the time table was strictly observed.

(3) That I was present in the room in which I was authorized to preside during the whole period of the examination, and that no other person was present except the candidates during said period.

(4) That during the whole of the examination my undivided attention was given to my duties as presiding examiner, and that no part of my time was taken up with any other duties whatsoever.

(5) That I made no suggestion to the candidates regarding the meaning of any question, or the kind of answer that they should give.

Presiding examiners are paid the sum of $4 per day and actual travelling expenses. The fees paid by the candidates for the examination are supposed to cover all the expenses of the presiding examiner, the necessary stationery, and the reading of the answers of the candidates.

Reading Answer Papers.—When the answer papers of candidates are received by the department they are classified according to subjects by the officers of the department. As the members of the committee appointed to read the answer papers in most cases are the teachers by whom the candidates were prepared for the examination, it is necessary to take all reasonable precautions for preventing the identification by the examiner of his own pupils. Accordingly, the slip placed on the envelope by the candidate which bore his name is removed, and the number by which the candidate was registered is placed upon his envelope, and as the departmental register in which the names of candidates are entered is confidential, there is no way of identifying a candidate except by his handwriting. When several thousand candidates send in papers, identification in this way is very improbable.

The examiners are classified in sections according to the subjects of examination. A member of the committee who prepared the examination papers acts as chairman of each section, or, if unable to act, a suitable person for that purpose is appointed by the joint board.

Before commencing the actual work of examination the examiners of each section are required to spend sufficient time in discussing the answers and reading answer papers jointly, to enable them to arrive at a consensus of opinion as to the valuation of answers, especially of partial or imperfect answers.

When a section finds that the values assigned to the questions on the examination papers are unsatisfactory, or when it is evident that the examiner did not follow the course of study prescribed by the Education Department or by the curriculum of the University of Toronto, the section shall report through its chairman to the chairman of the examiners or the person acting on his behalf.

In reading the papers each examiner is required to mark distinctly in the left-hand margin the value assigned by him to each answer or partial answer, and to sum up the total on each page at the foot of the margin, and to place the result on the face of the envelope, indicating the deductions for misspelled words and incorrect English thereon—thus, e. g., history 80 — 2 sp. — 4 f. s. (false syntax) = 74, and initialing the envelope of each paper examined.

In order that the examiners may maintain the necessary freshness and vigour for the duties to which they are appointed, they are limited to six hours of work per day, three hours in the forenoon, from nine to twelve, and three hours in the afternoon, from two to five. They are paid the sum of $6 per day, the payment being subject to the restriction that the whole amount paid for the examination shall not exceed the sum of $1.50 per candidate. In addition to this they are allowed actual railway expenses to and from their residences. In appraising the work of the candidates they are guided by the marks assigned to each subject by the Education Department. As the examination proceeds, the marks assigned to each candidate are entered by the registrar in a book prepared for that purpose. Candidates writing for third-class standing are required to obtain one third of the marks in each subject and one half of the aggregate. Candidates writing for second- or first- class standing are required to obtain only one third in each subject.

As soon as the registrar has completed the summing up of the marks awarded, his books are submitted to the committee appointed to prepare the examination papers. If a candidate has failed by a very few marks in a subject, but is on the whole a strong candidate, the committee is at liberty to recommend such candidate for full standing. After considering the work of the examiners and any special circumstances affecting the standing of any candidate, the results are reported to the joint board. On the acceptance of the report by the joint board, a list of candidates who have passed for matriculation is transmitted to the registrar of the university, and a list of candidates who have passed for first-, second-, or third-class standing is transmitted to the Minister of Education. Should any candidate be dissatisfied with the result of the examination, he may appeal within a certain time to the Minister of Education for a rereading of his papers. If his appeal is entertained, his answer papers are submitted for a rereading to the committee by whom the examination papers were prepared, which has full power to revise the work of the examiner in the first instance, and to consider such representations as may have been made with regard to sickness, or the unavoidable absence of the candidate from the examination.

In order to protect candidates from loss of standing through illness or any other incidental cause, the department requires every high-school master sending up candidates to the examination to transmit to the department confidentially a list of the candidates classified according to merit on the basis of such examinations as the high school may have conducted during the term. This list is submitted to the examiners, and is considered by them conjointly with the marks obtained by the candidate at the departmental examination. Should it appear that the candidate was ranked by the high school staff very high, and that the estimate of the staff with regard to other candidates was warranted by the results of the examinations generally, the ranking of the staff is accepted in lieu of the standing obtained by the candidate at the departmental examination. This mode of adjusting results has passed candidates who would otherwise have been rejected by the examiners, and is besides a reasonable protection to a good candidate from the consequence of a casual attack of illness, which might otherwise deprive him of the fruits of a year's labour.

CHAPTER VI.

TRAINING OF TEACHERS.

THERE are three different kinds of schools for the training of teachers under the public-school system of the Province of Ontario, viz., county model schools for teachers of third-class standing, normal schools for teachers of second- or first-class standing, and a normal training college, formerly called the School of Pedagogy, for persons holding a degree from a university in the British dominions, or such persons as have obtained first-class literary standing at the departmental examination and who intend to become teachers in a high school or collegiate institute.

In providing so fully for the training of teachers, the Education Department has proceeded upon the principle that no person should be allowed to take charge of a school without instruction in the theory and practice of teaching, and that to know a subject from the standpoint of a pupil is a very different thing from knowing it from the standpoint of a teacher.

As has already been noted, the department dissociates the literary course of study required for teachers, commonly called the nonprofessional course, from that subsequently required in pedagogics known as the professional course. It is not necessary here to discuss whether candidates for the teaching profession are better qualified by taking these two courses conjointly, or by taking them separately, as is done in the Province of Ontario. In the provincial normal school both courses were taken together for about thirty years, with very satisfactory results; for the last twenty years they have been taken separately, with equally satisfactory results as to the literary attainments of the candidates, and, it is believed, with better results as to their professional attainments. At the same time the secondary schools have been greatly stimulated and their usefulness increased by the presence in their class-rooms of young men and women preparing for the literary standing required for teachers.

County Model Schools.

By the School Act of 1871 provision was made for the appointment of a public-school inspector in each county, or, where the counties were very large, for the appointment of more inspectors than one. By the Act of 1877 provision was made for the establishment of a model school in every inspectoral division, and no person was thereafter allowed to enter the teaching profession unless he attended a term at the model school and passed the prescribed examination.

The county model school, subject to the regulations of the Education Department, is under the direction of a Board of Examiners, of whom the inspector is one, and not more than two other persons holding first-class certificates of qualification appointed by the Municipal Council of the county. The Board of Examiners is authorized to select from among the large public schools in the county or inspectoral district the particular school which in its opinion will best serve the purpose of a model school for the training of teachers. Usually the school in some incorporated village or town having the largest number of teachers, and the most easily accessible to the district, is selected. A school so established receives a special grant from the provincial treasury, and also from the county, in addition to all ordinary school grants.

The model school opens on the 1st of September and continues four months. No teacher is admitted to the county model school who has not passed at least the examination required for third-class literary standing, and who will be not less than eighteen years of age at the time of the final examination.

In order to guarantee the efficiency of the model school the department requires : 1. That the principal shall hold a first-class certificate—i. e., a certificate of the highest grade issued by the Education Department—and shall have had at least three years' experience as a public-school teacher. 2. That not fewer than three of the assistants on the staff of the school shall hold at least second-class certificates. 3. That the equipment of the school shall be in every respect satisfactory to the Education Department. 4. That in addition to the number of rooms required for the public school, a separate room shall be available for the teachers in training during their attendance at the model school. 5. That during the model-school term the principal shall be relieved of all public-school duties except the oversight of his staff.

It will be observed that a county model school is therefore presumably the best and largest public school in the inspectoral division, with a principal of considerable experience and high professional attainments, with a well-organized staff, and with all the other equipments and appliances necessary to the efficiency of a good school.

Every teacher in training is required to provide himself with a set of all the text-books used in the public school, and with such other books as may be required for training purposes.

Course of Study.—The course of study in county model schools consists of (*a*) instruction in school organization and management based on Baldwin's Art of School Management adapted to Canadian schools; (*b*) a course of lectures in the methodology of all the subjects taught in the public schools; (*c*) practice teaching with a view to the establishment of correct methods of presenting subjects to a class and of developing the art of school government; (*d*) a course in physiology and school sanitation; (*e*) instruction in the school law and regulations relating to the duties of teachers and pupils; (*f*) special instruction in music for primary classes; and (*g*) drill and calisthenics.

During the first six weeks of the term the work of the model school consists of (*a*) lectures by the principal; (*b*) class teaching by the principal; (*c*) class teaching by the students, and general criticism. After the first two or three lectures by the principal, classes are drafted from the public school, by means of which the principal of the model school illustrates his method of teaching the subject to which he wishes to direct the attention of the teachers in training. This done, the principal assigns a lesson for class teaching by the model-school students, which any student, if called upon, shall be expected to teach the following day—the other students to take notes for subsequent criticism. For six weeks, by means of lectures and class teaching by the principal and the students, with appropriate criticisms, the teachers have acquired enlarged powers of observation, greater confidence in themselves, and some conception of the logical order in which a subject should be presented to a class.

During the remainder of the term the time of the teachers in training is divided between lectures by the principal, observing methods of teaching in the different rooms of the public school to which the model school is attached, and in teaching such subjects as may be assigned to them. Every teacher in training before conducting a recitation in the public school is required to prepare a plan of the lesson which he is to teach, and to submit the same for the approval of the principal or assistant in charge of the class. While teaching, the assistant or principal is required to take notes of the work of the teacher in training, such as his attitude before his class, his mode of presenting the subject—whether logical or otherwise—his mode of questioning the pupils and of dealing with their answers, his mode of explaining difficulties—whether clear and complete or otherwise, etc. These criticisms are made known to the teacher in training privately, or are made the subject of a lecture by the principal for the benefit of the whole class at a later stage.

A small reference library is provided for each model school by the Education Department, consisting of such books as are considered most helpful in preparing teachers for their work, and in increasing their knowledge of education, both as a science and an art.

Final Examinations.—The final examination consists of practical teaching by the teachers in training in presence of the Board of Examiners, and also a written examination on papers submitted by the Education Department. The examination in practical teaching consists of two lessons of twenty minutes each, for one of which the teacher is allowed ample time for preparation; the other is assigned forty minutes before it is to be taught. These two lessons are not to be taught in the same form, nor in the same subject, nor before the same examiners.

As the examiner is either the inspector or an experienced teacher of the highest standing, he is fully qualified to pronounce judgment upon every teacher in training that comes before him. By personal observation he can form an opinion as to his manner before his pupils, his force of character, his power to command attention, and the many other elements only perceptible to an experienced eye and ear, which are essential to a teacher's success and to his influence over his pupils. These qualities he appraises according to a scale of one hundred marks. If the candidate falls below fifty marks he is rejected, and is required to attend another session if he still desires to enter the profession.

The written examination is conducted on papers prepared under the direction of the Education Department by a committee of inspectors or teachers of the highest standing. These papers are printed by the confidential printer of the department, are transmitted under seal to the inspector, and are given out to the teachers in training according to a time table prepared by the department. The answers of the candidates are read by the Board of Examiners and appraised according to the standard of marks assigned to each paper by the department.

In order to protect the candidate at his professional examination, as has already been indicated with regard to the literary examination, the Examiners consider, conjointly with the examination which they are authorized to conduct, a report from the principal of the school with regard to the standing of every teacher in training during the term, and on the strength of these three different estimates of his attainments—viz., teaching in their own presence, the answers of the written papers, and the report of the principal and assistants of the model school—a candidate is passed or rejected. There is no appeal from the decision of the board.

Candidates who have passed this examination are known as the holders of third-class certificates, and are qualified to teach any public school in the province for a period of three years. The Board of Examiners has, however, the power of extending this certificate where the supply of teachers is inadequate, or for other sufficient reason, subject to the approval of the Minister of Education.

After eighteen years' experience of the working of county model schools, it is the universal opinion of the profession in Ontario that the training, even elementary and limited as it is, is invaluable to the young teacher. His knowledge of the philosophy of education may not be very extensive; he may not even have acquired sufficient knowledge of school organization to classify properly a large ungraded school; but he has, however, learned the necessity of teaching according to some preconceived design or lesson plan, of guarding against all unprofessional peculiarities which might mar his usefulness, of practising self-control and personal dignity before a class, of cultivating the attentive interest of his pupils, and of presenting his own thoughts with clearness, fluency, and animation. When he takes charge of a school for the first time, he knows what to do, and within certain limitations how to do it, and consequently avoids the mistakes of a teacher wholly inexperienced. He has also become acquainted with a wider field of professional literature, and is impressed with the necessity of higher educational attainments. In many cases the professional *esprit de corps*, aroused at the county model school, has been the means of leading the young teacher to professional eminence. The county model school has certainly secured for Ontario a system of preliminary training for teachers at once effective and inexpensive.

NORMAL SCHOOLS.

As far back as 1843 the Legislative Assembly of Ontario contemplated the establishment of one or more normal schools in the province, but it was not until 1846 that a sufficient amount of money was placed at the disposal of the Education Department for that purpose, and on the 1st day of November, 1847, the first normal school in the province was formally opened in the city of Toronto, with an attendance of twenty students, which increased during the session to sixty-one.

Owing to the removal of Parliament to Montreal, the residence of the Lieutenant-Governor was vacant, and was placed at the disposal of the Government for normal-school purposes. The stables attached to Government House were fitted up for the model school, which was opened on the 21st of February, 1848, with an attendance of one hundred and twenty pupils. When Parliament returned to Toronto, in 1849, the normal school was transferred to the Temperance Hall in Temperance Street, and in 1852 was removed to its present quarters in St. James's Square.

For thirty years the normal school provided the only professional training available to the teachers of the province, and as it was capable of accommodating only one hundred and twenty students, the number of trained teachers in the profession was necessarily very limited. The other members of the profession (and they were greatly in the majority) entered upon their duties without any professional training whatsoever, and at the cost of their pupils acquired such skill in methods and school management as enabled them to remain in the profession for a few years.

A second normal school was opened in the city of Ottawa, in the eastern part of the province, in 1875, and it is hoped that before long a third will be opened in the western part of the province. With three normal schools, the course of professional training required of teachers with second-class literary standing would be amply provided for.

Organization of Normal Schools.—The normal schools of Ontario consist of two departments, viz., one for the instruction of teachers in training, and the other—a model or practice school for illustrating methods of teaching. The normal-school staff consists of a principal and vice-principal, and four other teachers, viz., one for each of the following: drawing, music, drill and calisthenics, and kindergarten work.

Before a teacher can be admitted to a provincial normal school (*a*) he must have passed the examinations of the county model school, (*b*) he must have taught successfully one year, and (*d*) he must have attained second-class literary standing. He is also required to pass a preliminary examination orally and in writing on the following texts: Hopkins's Outline Study of Man, the first seven lectures; Quick's Educational Reformers, the first sixteen chapters; Fitch's Lectures on Teaching, the first five lectures. The object of this preliminary examination is to direct the attention of the teacher to the necessity of private reading while engaged professionally, and to prepare him for receiving more readily the instruction of the normal-school staff.

The normal schools are nonresidential, but the houses

at which the students lodge are inspected, and no student is permitted to lodge except at a licensed boarding house or with some relative or friend. Gentlemen attending the normal school must lodge in boarding houses not attended by the other sex. Students are liable to discipline for any irregularity while attending the normal school. In the classrooms the sexes are instructed together; outside the classrooms they are allowed reasonable intercourse with each other, it being assumed that their conduct would be such as would characterize ladies and gentlemen in good society.

The practice or model school is immediately connected with the building used for normal-school purposes, and is divided into classes corresponding to the number of forms in the public school. For convenience of administration, the sexes are separated in the model school. An opportunity is afforded by this arrangement of testing the capacity of the students for handling classes of boys and girls when taken separately. Each normal school has ample playgrounds for the use of the pupils and the teachers in training, a suitable gymnasium for drill and calisthenics, and a reference library of several thousand volumes. The average cost of maintaining a normal and model school is about $24,000 annually.

Course of Study.—The course of study in the normal school is mainly professional, and includes the history of education, science of education, school organization and management, methods of teaching each subject on the public-school course, practice in managing classes, and in teaching in the model school, with special instruction in reading, writing, drawing, music, drill and calisthenics, and lectures on hygiene and school sanitation. In conjunction with these lectures, teachers in training are required to study carefully the following texts: Quick's Educational Reformers (introduction by Dr. Harris) McLellan's Applied Psychology, and Fitch's Lectures on Teaching.

As in county model schools, the object of the course of study at the normal school is to present every subject from the standpoint of the teacher rather than to increase the student's knowledge of the subject itself, and as the examinations, at the close of the session, deal entirely with methods of instruction, the teachers in training are free to give their undivided attention to the professional side of their education.

On every Friday afternoon classes for religious instruction are formed, in which the teachers in training receive instruction from a clergyman of their own denomination. This instruction is given without charge by the resident clergymen of the city.

In practical teaching the course of study is similar to that in the county model school, but on a higher plane. Model lessons are given by the staff to classes of pupils drafted from the model school; the teachers in training teach lessons previously assigned to them in the presence of the staff and of their fellow-teachers in training; after observing the methods of the model school, they are required to teach in the presence of the principal or of the teachers in charge. These lessons are the basis of subsequent criticism, and thus from day to day by actual practice they are acquiring a wider knowledge and a deeper experience with respect to their professional duties.

Examinations.—A written report with regard to the standing of each teacher in training is transmitted by the principal to the Minister of Education at the close of the term. The final examination consists of a test in practical teaching by examiners appointed by the Minister of Education, and a written examination on the subjects of the course. The mode of conducting the practical examination is briefly as follows:

1. Each teacher in training shall teach two lessons before the examiners appointed by the Minister of Education.

2. The examiners shall, on consultation with the teachers of the model school, assign the lessons to the teachers in training. The two lessons shall not be assigned in the same form or in the same subject.

3. The subject of the first lesson shall be given by the presiding examiner to the teacher in training the day before, and the subject of the second lesson forty minutes before the lesson is to be taught.

4. After a lesson has been assigned no hint or assistance of any kind shall be given to the teacher in training by any examiner or teacher on the staff of the normal or model school.

5. Each teacher in training shall be allowed twenty minutes in which to teach the lesson assigned.

6. The regular teacher in charge of the room shall not be present during the teaching of a test lesson.

7. The examiner shall, on the basis of one hundred marks, appraise the aptitude and efficiency of each teacher in training, and in all doubtful cases shall set forth in writing the reasons for the marks assigned.

8. At the close of the examination the examiner shall report the standing of each teacher in training to the Minister of Education.

The papers for the written examination are prepared by a committee of public-school inspectors or other educational experts, who read the answers and report the results to the Minister of Education. These papers are printed by the confidential printer of the Education Department.

The final standing of candidates is determined upon the conjoint report of the principal and his staff, the practical examination by the examiners appointed by the minister, and the written examination referred to. Where the staff reports that a teacher in training is beyond question devoid of teaching power, and unfitted for the profession, such candidate is rejected by the Education Department and refused his standing. He is at liberty, however, to attend another session. Candidates who pass the examination are awarded a second-class certificate, valid during good behaviour, in any part of the province.

Kindergarten Teachers.

The kindergarten was introduced into the Province of Ontario in 1882 under a clause in the School Act authorizing trustees to establish infant schools. It was not until 1885, however, that suitable provision was made for the instruction of kindergarten teachers by the establishment of a practice school in connection with each of the normal schools under the direction of a trained kindergartner.

The course of training for kindergarten teachers covers a period of two years—one year for an assistant, and an additional year for a director. No person is admitted to the course of study prescribed for assistants (*a*) who is not seventeen years of age, (*b*) who has not passed the examination required for third-class literary standing, or (*c*) who has not received at least three years' instruction in a high school or collegiate institute. The standing of an assistant must be obtained before the course of study prescribed for a director can be taken up.

Kindergartens are under the control of the Education Department, and are part of the public-school system. Every kindergarten opened by a Board of Trustees is under a director holding a certificate from the Education Department.

Persons desiring to train themselves as kindergarten teachers spend the first year of their course as an assistant under a qualified director. At the conclusion of the first year's course of training they must be able to explain the Gifts, their general objects as well as their specialties; how they are graded and why; their connection with other branches of kindergarten work; also the general method of the kindergarten, and how applied in exercises with the gifts. As the gifts have a mathematical foundation, a knowledge of the elements of geometry will be required. Assistants are also required to know how to explain the general objects of the songs and games, the significance of gesture used in connection with them, and to show by what principles they should be guided in the selection of songs, games, and stories. They must possess a knowledge of elementary science, particularly of animals, plants, earth, air, water, etc., and be able to illustrate the interesting portions of these subjects in stories and conversation with the children.

At the end of one year's service they are subjected to an examination conducted by the department in the theory and practice of the gifts, the theory and practice of the occupations, and a miscellaneous paper testing their general knowledge on subjects relating to kindergarten work. They are also required to submit the book work of the year for the inspection of the examiners. They are then admitted to one of the provincial kindergartens established in connection with the normal schools, and at the end of the second year are subjected to an examination on the general principles of Froebel's System, the theory and practice of the gifts and occupations, Mutter und Koselieder, and practical teaching. A miscellaneous paper on matters connected with kindergarten work is also required at this examination. The examination is conducted by examiners appointed by the Minister of Education. Candidates who pass the examination for directors are qualified to take charge of any kindergarten in the province.

The director of the provincial kindergarten gives instruction to the teachers in training at the normal school in kindergarten occupations, songs, and games. In this way every teacher who passes through a normal school for an ordinary certificate obtains a general knowledge of kindergarten work and methods. The number of kindergartens in Ontario in 1894 was 90, the number of teachers 184, and the number of pupils 9,340.

NORMAL TRAINING COLLEGE.

The Education Department, encouraged by the success of the training of teachers for public schools, was led to make similar provision for the training of teachers in high schools and collegiate institutes. The necessity for this was the more urgent because, by the abandonment of all nonprofessional work in the normal schools, it was necessary that the high schools and collegiate institutes, where the future teachers of public schools received their literary instruction, should be conducted by men and women well grounded in pedagogical science. Moreover, it was felt that if the professional training of a teacher was of advantage in the elementary work of the public school, there was no reason why it should not prove helpful to teachers of secondary schools. The psychological principles which apply to the development of the child's mind in the early stages of his education apply to his development in all other stages. To require the teacher who had to lay the foundation of a child's education to be trained for that work and then to transfer the child to teachers who had no training, involved a lack of continuity in method and in development which could not fail to be injurious to his higher education.

Accordingly, in 1885, several of the best collegiate institutes of the province were set apart as training institutes at which candidates for standing as high-school teachers were required to attend for about five months in the year in order to observe the methods of experienced teachers, and to receive such instruction from the principal as he could conveniently give, without interfering with his other duties.

Elementary and limited as this preliminary training was, it justified the department in establishing a School of Pedagogy with a regular staff appointed by the department for the special training of high-school masters. For several years the school was conducted without any practice school. As a substitute for classes of pupils, the teachers in training were themselves constituted a class, and their powers of developing a lesson tested by practising on each other, in the presence of the principal and his staff. The want of a practice school was greatly felt, and so, following out the principle on which county model schools were organized, the School of Pedagogy is hereafter to be attached to one of the largest collegiate institutes in the province, and its name changed to that of "Normal College." By this means the teacher in training will receive the benefit of the experience of at least sixteen trained teachers, and have an opportunity of studying methods in a practice school of over six hundred pupils. Separate classrooms, waiting rooms, lavatories, and private rooms are to be provided for the students and the official staff, in addition to those required by the pupils of the school. The gymnasium of the institute and its physical and chemical laboratories are also available for the students of the college when required.

In all collegiate institutes in the province the leading subjects of study, such as classics, moderns, etc., are in charge of specialists—i. e., of men who have taken honours at their university prior to their appointment, and who, either by experience or by training at the School of Pedagogy have earned this rank. In order, therefore, to place the students of the Normal College under the most favourable conditions for their development, all the Education Department has to do is to appoint a principal and one or more assistants to give the necessary instruction in psychology, the history of education, school organization and management in the Normal College proper, and to arrange with the teachers of the collegiate institute for instruction in the methodology of the various subjects on the high-school course of study. For these services and the accommodation already mentioned the Education Department pays the trustees of the collegiate institute the sum of $2,500 per annum.

The Normal Training College opens on the 1st of October and closes on the 31st of May. No preliminary written examination is required, and no fees, except an examination fee of ten dollars. Before a student can be admitted to the Training College he must possess first-class literary standing, or be an undergraduate of the fourth year of a university in the British dominions, or the holder of a degree in arts. As it is considered important that teachers should not be placed in charge of a high school until they have reached some maturity, it is provided that no student shall be admitted to the Training College who will not have attained twenty-one years of age on or before the close of the session.

Students are required to lodge and board at such houses only as are approved by the principal. Ladies and gentlemen shall not board at the same house. Communication between the sexes is prohibited except by permission of the principal or one of his staff. Students are required to attend regularly and punctually throughout the session, and to submit to such discipline and to perform such duties as may be required by the principal.

Courses of Study and Text-books.—1. The course of study and training shall be as follows : Psychology; the history and criticism of educational systems ; the science of education; lectures with practical illustrations of the best method of teaching each subject on the programme of studies for high schools; lectures on school organization and management; observation and practice teaching ; instruction in reading, physiology, and temperance, writing, drawing, and stenography; drill, gymnastics, and calisthenics for male teachers; drill and calisthenics for female teachers; and such other subjects as may be prescribed by the Minister of Education.

2. In addition to the text-books prescribed for high schools, the following are used in the School of Pedagogy: Quick's Essays on Educational Reformers (International Education Series, 1890 edition), McLellan's Applied Psychology, Spencer's Education, Landon's School Management, Fitch's Lectures on Teaching, Manual of Hygiene, Infantry Drill, as revised by her Majesty's command (edition of 1892)—for male teachers, Parts I and II, and for

female teachers, Part I, pages 1-31; for male and female teachers, Houghton's Physical Culture (omitting squad drill); and, for male teachers, MacLaren's Physical Education, Part II, sections 2 and 3.

3. The following are recommended for reference: Mahaffy's Old Greek Education, Compayré's History of Pedagogy, Gill's Systems of Education, Radestock's Habit in Education, Dewey's Psychology, Sully's Teacher's Handbook of Psychology (Appleton), and Ladd's Outlines of Physiological Psychology.

The Teaching Staff.—The principal is the chief instructor in the theoretical and critical course, and is responsible for the organization and management of the school. He determines the hours for instruction, observation, and practice teaching; he prescribes the duties of his staff, and is expected to observe the practice teaching of the students.

Each assistant is required to develop systematically the best method of dealing with the special objects intrusted to him, and to explain and justify his methods on scientific principles, giving model lessons for classes in the different stages of their advancement. He is also to criticise the practice teaching of the students, and to keep a record of their standing.

Examinations.—The students are submitted to two written examinations during the session, one in December and the other in March. These examinations are conducted by the staff of the school, and the results reported to the Minister of Education at the close of the session. No certificate is awarded to any student against whom the staff reports on account of deficient teaching ability. At the close of the session, a written examination is held by examiners appointed by the Minister of Education. The papers for this examination are prepared by special examiners appointed by the minister, and certificates are awarded on the joint result of the final examination and the report of the teaching staff.

Following the methods of the German gymnasium, the certificates awarded to students who pass the examination of the Training College are interim certificates— i. e., the holder is authorized to teach as an assistant in a high school for two years. At the end of that time, if the high-school inspector reports to the Minister of Education that the holder of such certificate has proved successful as a teacher, the Minister of Education makes the interim certificate permanent during good behaviour.

Specialists.—Students who have attained university honours before entering the Normal Training College and who have passed the examinations required by the Education Department are awarded the standing of specialists in the department in which they obtained honours. This qualifies them to become teachers of classics, modern languages, mathematics, or science in a collegiate institute. Those without this standing are qualified only as teachers in high schools or in the subordinate departments of a collegiate institute.

Teachers' Institutes.—In order to maintain a professional *esprit de corps* among teachers and also to bring them more closely into sympathy with current opinion respecting their work and duty, the Education Department provides for the holding of a Teachers' Institute in every inspectoral division once a year. For the purpose of attending these institutes, the teachers are relieved from school two regular teaching days in the year, without being required to ask permission from their trustees. Any teacher who absents himself from the institute must report to his inspector the reasons for his absence.

The Teachers' Institute is organized by the appointment of a president, vice-president, and secretary-treasurer, with a management committee of five. At least one meeting of the institute must be held every year, extending over two or more days. The management committee is to provide a programme and to send a copy of the same to every teacher in the inspectoral division, at least one month before the time of meeting. The subjects to be discussed are determined by the committee of management; the only limitation laid upon the committee by the department is that all questions and discussions foreign to the teachers' work shall be avoided. In order to encourage the attendance of trustees, a portion of the afternoon of the second day's session is set apart for considering matters affecting the relation of teachers and trustees. Boards of trustees are allowed to pay the travelling expenses of one representative from each board for attendance at such meetings. The inspector of the county is required to be present at all meetings of the Teachers' Institute. He is eligible for appointment as president or as a member of the management committee, but unless so appointed his position as inspector gives him no more authority than that possessed by any other member of the institute.

Every Teachers' Institute is expected to establish a reference library for the benefit of its members, and receives for this purpose annually the sum of twenty-five dollars from the County Council and an equal sum from the provincial treasury. An officer of the department, appointed for that purpose, visits every institute once in two years to discuss with the teachers such questions as the board of management may suggest, or as may be considered important by the director in the interests of education. Usually the subjects discussed by the director are settled by consultation with the Minister of Education. Should it appear from the reports of the inspectors that any subject in the public-school course of study is neglected or badly taught, or should there be any apathy among teachers with regard to any department of school work, the Director of Institutes, in a suitable address, calls their attention to the subject so neglected, indicating the defects to be remedied, and enforcing his admonitions by departmental authority. The director is also required to deliver a popular address in the town or city in which the institute holds its meeting. The subject of this address is chosen with a view to increase the interest of the ratepayers in education, to encourage them in supporting more liberally and sympathetically teachers whom they employ, and to correct such misapprehensions as might be known to exist with regard to courses of study; the regulations of the department or the value of education in the development of a higher national life.

CHAPTER VII.

HIGH SCHOOLS AND COLLEGIATE INSTITUTES.

GRAMMAR schools, now known as high schools or collegiate institutes, occupy a midway position between the public school and the university. Although the courses of the public school and the high school [*] overlap as to one form, generally speaking, it may be said that where the public-school course ends the high-school course begins, and, with a similar reservation, where the high-school course ends the university course begins. By means of examinations conducted by the Education Department an organic connection is maintained between these three divisions of the school system of Ontario.

History.—It has already been noted that in 1807 a public school was established in each of the eight districts into which the province was divided, and the sum of $400 appropriated by Parliament for the maintenance of each school. The schools authorized by this act were as follows: One in Sandwich; one in Townsend, in the county of Norfolk; one in Niagara; one in York (now Toronto);

---

[*] To avoid repetition the term "high school" will be used as the equivalent of the double term "high school and collegiate institute." A collegiate institute is simply a large high school possessing a staff specially trained to give instruction in classics, moderns, mathematics, science, and commercial work.

one in the township of Hamilton, in the county of Northumberland; one in Kingston; one in the township of Augusta; and one in the town of Cornwall. As these schools were about one hundred miles apart, it will be seen what limited facilities for the education of the people were considered necessary about a century ago. It should not be forgotten, however, that private schools, as local necessities warranted, were established at other places, some of them conducted by men with a university education and for moderate fees. Of all the private schools opened during this period, the most successful was the one at Cornwall, under Dr. John Strachan, afterward Bishop of Toronto.

The first grammar school—or, more properly speaking, public school—in the Province of Ontario was opened in York (now Toronto) on the 1st of June, 1807; the second in Niagara in 1808.

By an amendment made in 1819 to the original act of 1807 the trustees of every school district were required to hold a public examination previous to the annual vacation, and to report the standing of the schools and the number of pupils in attendance to the Lieutenant-Governor. Provision was also made in the same act for the free education of ten indigent pupils, should there be as many in each district. The school established in the township of Augusta was transferred to Brockville, and an additional school opened in Hamilton. In 1837 the school established in the township of Townsend was transferred to London.

In 1839 district public schools were first called "grammar schools," and two hundred and fifty thousand acres of the waste lands of the Crown set apart for the purpose of providing a fund for their maintenance. Authority was

HIGH SCHOOLS AND COLLEGIATE INSTITUTES. 113

given the Government to pay the sum of $800 for the erection of school buildings in each district, provided an equal sum was voluntarily contributed by the inhabitants. Provision was also made for the establishment of two additional schools in the district where suitable schoolhouses were provided by the people and an attendance of not less than sixty scholars guaranteed. The most important provision, however, of the Act of 1839 was the placing of the grammar schools under the administration of the Council of King's College,* with authority to the Council " to make such rules, regulations, and by-laws for the conduct and good government of the schools established under this act as to such Council shall seem proper."

In 1841 the powers vested in the Council of King's College with respect to the supervision and administration of grammar schools were transferred to the Executive Government of the province, and provision made for the investment of any funds that might accrue from the sale of lands set apart for grammar-school purposes under the Act of 1839.

In 1853—through the instrumentality of Dr. Ryerson, then Chief Superintendent of Education for the Province of Ontario—important amendments were made to the Grammar School Act, of which the following are worthy of special notice:

1. Municipal Councils were authorized to levy a rate upon the taxable property of the district for the erection of high-school buildings, the purchase of school apparatus and text-books, and the payment of teachers' salaries.

2. The course of study was for the first time regulated

---

* King's College was the name given to the first university established in Ontario.

by act of Parliament. This course consisted of instruction "in the higher branches of a practical English and commercial education, including the elements of natural philosophy and mechanics and also the Latin and Greek languages and mathematics, so far as to prepare students for matriculation into the University of Toronto or any college affiliated with the University of Toronto."

3. The Council of Public Instruction was authorized to define this course of study, to frame rules and regulations for the government of the schools, and to prescribe the text-books to be used by the pupils. The President of the University of Toronto and the president or other head of all colleges affiliated with the University of Toronto were made members of the Council of Public Instruction for grammar-school purposes.

4. Trustees of high schools were henceforth to be appointed by the Municipal Council of the county in which the high school was situated, and authority given them to appoint such masters as might be necessary and to dismiss them as they might deem expedient.

5. No person was eligible to be appointed master of a grammar school who did not hold a degree from some university or a certificate of qualification from a board of examiners appointed by the Council of Public Instruction. The Principal of the Normal School was, by statute, a member of this Board of Examiners.

7. County Councils were authorized to establish additional grammar schools, providing the fund at the disposal of the Government for that purpose would sustain a charge of $200 for each new school after paying $400 to all schools previously established.

8. Certain grammar schools were set apart as meteorological stations, and the principal of the school was

HIGH SCHOOLS AND COLLEGIATE INSTITUTES. 115

supplied with scientific appliances for taking observations with regard to the fall of rain, direction and velocity of the wind, the pressure and temperature of the atmosphere, etc. For these services an allowance of $180 a year for each school so constituted was made by the Provincial Government.

The chief features of the Act of 1853 summed up are :

(*a*) That the appointment of high-school trustees was transferred from the Executive Government, where it was placed by the Act of 1807, to County Councils.

(*b*) That high-school masters were appointed by the trustees directly, and not nominated as under the Act of 1807 for the approval of the Executive Government.

(*c*) That the Education Department of the province was invested with similar powers with regard to grammar schools as it possessed with regard to public schools.

(*d*) That grammar schools were regarded as a distinct part of the school system of the province with a well-defined course of instruction, and entitled to support by a Government tax upon property.

(*e*) That the legal obligation was imposed upon them of preparing students for matriculation into the provincial university.

In 1855 the act was amended, authorizing the Education Department to establish a model grammar school for the training of high-school masters, and to appoint an inspector of grammar schools.

In 1865 the Board of Examiners for granting certificates to masters of grammar schools was abolished, and thereafter no person should be deemed qualified to be appointed principal of a grammar school unless he was a graduate of some university within the British dominions. Provision was also made for a course of elementary military instruction at high schools, and for the payment of a grant of $50 to any school the principal of which was qualified to give such instruction as would be satisfactory to the Executive Government.

In 1871 the term "high school" was to be applied to the schools previously constituted "grammar schools," and a Board of Examiners was constituted for the admission of pupils to high schools. The French and German languages were added to the course of study, and high schools, with four masters specially qualified, were to be called collegiate institutes.

This brief historical outline leads to the consideration of the present constitution of high schools in the province.

High Schools—how established.—The Municipal Council of any county may pass a by-law for the establishment of a high school in any municipality containing not fewer than one thousand inhabitants. The council of a city may establish more high schools than one, as it may deem expedient. All by-laws for the establishment of high schools are subject to the approval of the Executive Government. Ordinarily the municipality in which the high school is situated is the municipality responsible for its maintenance. Several municipalities, however, may unite for the purpose of maintaining a high school.

In the case of high schools situated in a city or town separate from the county, the Municipal Council appoints the trustees for the high schools. In the case of high schools otherwise situated, three of the trustees are appointed by the county and three by the local municipality. Where the high school consists of several municipalities, each municipality is represented by at least one trustee. Provision is made for the retirement of a certain number of trustees each year, so as to maintain the continuity of

HIGH SCHOOLS AND COLLEGIATE INSTITUTES. 117

the office of school trustee, as in the case of public schools. Any resident ratepayer, twenty-one years of age, who is not a member of the council of the municipality or county in which the high school is situated, shall be qualified to serve as a high-school trustee. The Board of Public School Trustees of any city, town, or incorporated village may unite with the Board of High School Trustees. In cases of such union, the public and high schools of the municipality are under the management of one board, called a Board of Education. This board possesses all the powers which the law confers upon public and high school trustees when acting as separate corporations.

Duties and Powers of Trustees.—The trustees have power to fix the time and place of their own meetings, the mode of calling and conducting them, and of keeping an account of the proceedings of such meetings. They have the power of engaging such teachers and other officers as may be required, of fixing their salaries, and of dismissing them as they may deem expedient. They have power to expel pupils whose conduct may be deemed injurious to the welfare of the school. They are required to provide adequate accommodation according to the regulations of the Education Department for all resident pupils, and to see that the high school is conducted according to law. They are required to keep the buildings in proper repair, and to provide such equipment as may be required by the Education Department. Any high-school trustee who enters into a contract with the corporation of which he is a member, or is convicted of any felony or misdemeanor, or becomes insane, or who absents himself from the meetings of the board for three months in succession without permission, *ipso facto*, vacates his seat. High-school trustees serve without any remuneration.

High School Sites and Buildings.—The trustees have authority to select a site for high schools without reference either to the ratepayers or to the Municipal Council. By the regulations of the department it is provided, however, that the site must be at least one half an acre in extent, easily accessible, with the grounds properly levelled and drained and fenced, planted with shade trees, and suitably provided with walks in front and rear. Closets for the sexes must be separate, in separate yards, and properly screened from observation. The playgrounds must be ample for physical exercise, and a proper supply of drinking water must be provided. The plans for new high schools are subject to the approval of the Education Department.

In a general way the department requires the class-rooms to be conveniently arranged and tasteful in appearance; well proportioned and oblong in shape; twelve square feet on the floor, and at least two hundred and fifty cubic feet of air space for each pupil; ceilings white; a suitable platform for the teacher's desk; in three or more masters' schools a special classroom for the teaching of science; in two masters' schools, provision for science teaching in one of the rooms; separate entrances to each classroom for the sexes, and separate means of egress to the closets. Separate halls, staircases, waiting rooms and cloak rooms of suitable size and of convenient arrangement, furnished with benches and cap hooks, etc., for the sexes, are also required.

In small schools a private room for the joint use of the staff, properly furnished, is all that is required; in large schools with large staffs a separate room for the assistant masters and for the female assistants is required. The desks, blackboards, heating, lighting, ventilation, and ap-

HIGH SCHOOLS AND COLLEGIATE INSTITUTES. 119

paratus are all subject to the inspection of the department, and schools deficient in these respects are either reported against and are liable to the loss of the entire Government grant, or the Government grant is cut down as the defects in the accommodation of the school would warrant.

High Schools, how sustained.—High schools are sustained from three different sources: (*a*) a Government grant, (*b*) rates upon the taxable property of the municipality, and (*c*) fees from pupils. The Government grant consists of (*a*) a fixed sum of $375 to each high school; (*b*) a sum varying from $100 to $200 on the condition and suitability of the school premises; (*c*) a sum varying from $100 to $200 on the value of the equipment (this includes the library, physical and chemical apparatus, maps and globes, and gymnasium); (*d*) ten per cent on the amount expended on teachers' salaries over $1,500, but so as not to exceed $600 to any school; (*e*) a small sum is also paid on the basis of average attendance, and the sum of $275 is annually allowed each collegiate institute as a grant for equipment.

The sum voted by the Legislature is divided, with a view to encourage the improvement of the school premises, the equipment of the school, and the employment of teachers of the highest standing. The advancement of the high schools within the last ten years is ample proof of the stimulating effect of this mode of dividing the school grant.*

Trustees may require the Municipal Council to provide

---

* The annual grant by the Legislature of the province, in 1895, for high-school purposes, was $100,000; but this sum is subject to increase or decrease, as the Legislature may deem expedient.

such sums in addition to the Government grant as may be necessary for the maintenance of high schools. Prior to 1871 the Municipal Council was not obliged to impose a rate for high-school purposes at the request of the trustees; now they can not refuse. A board of trustees can not, however, raise money for the erection of a new high school without the consent of the Municipal Council, and if the Municipal Council decline, then the consent of the ratepayers by a vote taken for that purpose must be obtained. As all high schools, except those situated in cities and in towns separated from the county, are considered county schools, the Municipal Council of the county is obliged to pay for the maintenance of the high school a sum at least equal to the Government grant, or, at the request of the trustees, a sum equal to the cost of the instruction of a pupil at the high school. Owing to the wide area from which the high-school pupils are drawn, it would be unfair to tax the municipality in which the high school was situated for the benefit of the surrounding district. Municipalities, therefore, which do not establish a high school for their own benefit, are permitted to enjoy the advantage of the schools established elsewhere by simply paying the cost of instructing the pupils at such high school.

High School Fees.—High schools, unlike the public schools, are not free schools by law, although the trustees in cities, towns, and incorporated villages have power to make them free schools for pupils residing within the municipality. Pupils who are not residents of the municipality, but who live within the county, can not be charged a school fee higher than one dollar per month. In respect to resident pupils and pupils who live beyond the limits of the county in which the high school is situated, the trustees may either admit them free or impose such fees as they may deem expedient. As trustees appear to have a laudable ambition to have a large school, the fees imposed are usually very moderate. In 1895 the average for the province was a trifle less than five dollars per pupil.

Entrance Examination.—A uniform entrance examination for the admission of pupils to high schools is held annually at every high school, and at such other places as may be approved by the Education Department, and consists of an oral examination in reading and a written examination in literature, spelling, writing, geography, grammar, composition, history, and physiology and temperance.

The papers for the entrance examination are prepared by the inspectors of the high schools, assisted by such other examiners as may be appointed by the Minister of Education. These papers are printed by the confidential printer of the Education Department and transmitted to the public-school inspectors, who are, under the regulations, responsible for the proper conduct of the examination. The answer papers of the candidates are examined by a Board of Examiners consisting of the principal of the high school, the public-school inspector for the district, and one other person holding at least a second-class certificate with five years' experience as a teacher, appointed by the trustees of the public school and the trustees of the separate school respectively of the city, town, or incorporated village in which the high school is situated. The examiners are paid by the trustees of the high school at the rate of one dollar per pupil for conducting the examination and reading the answer papers of the candidates. Pupils who pass this examination receive a certificate signed by the inspector of public schools, which entitles them to admission to any high school in the province.

Courses of Study.—The high-school course of study is divided into four forms; each form is supposed to cover the work of one year. At the end of the third form, a high-school pupil should be qualified for matriculation into the university. The work of the fourth form corresponds as near as may be to the course of the first year at the university.

The subjects of the high-school course consist of—

1. English, including reading, grammar and rhetoric, composition, literature, history, and geography.

2. Language, including Latin, Greek, French, and German.

3. Mathematics, including arithmetic and mensuration, algebra, geometry, and trigonometry.

4. Science, including chemistry, physics, botany, and zoölogy.

5. Commercial work, including bookkeeping, stenography, and drawing.

English Course.—By the course in English a pupil is expected to acquire a thorough knowledge of etymology and syntax, the logical as well as the rhetorical structure of sentences and paragraphs, and an intelligent and appreciative comprehension of the best literature of the day. By means of a reference library established in connection with every high school, pupils are encouraged to acquaint themselves with the best writers of the English language, and, as the course in English is varied from year to year, every pupil who passes through a high school will be reasonably familiar with the works of all the great poets, such as Shakespeare, Milton, Cowper, Wordsworth, Byron, Scott, Coleridge, Longfellow, etc.

While it is the aim of the high school to cultivate correct standards, both as to writing and speaking, the minds of the pupils are at the same time directed to the form of expression which constitutes one of the chief beauties of English literature and to the refining influences which good literature should exert upon the mind and character. The study of literature expands from form to form, the pupil being constantly reminded as he proceeds that the examination in the first form, which was largely a test of the grammatical and rhetorical structure of his composition, will in the fourth form require a more comprehensive knowledge of the whole field of literature, a better vocabulary for the expression of his ideas, and more finish as to style and rhythm of composition.

Language.—In the first and second forms the study of language is optional, but the pupils are advised to begin the study of Latin and either French or German. In the second form they are advised to take up either the second classical or the second modern language. As pupils can matriculate into the university with a knowledge of three languages—i. e., the two classical languages and one modern, or Latin and two modern languages with physical science—the pupil makes a choice of his language course in the second form, and this choice is the basis of his course either for matriculation or for second-class literary standing as a teacher.

The language course includes a knowledge of grammar, the power to translate into English and *vice versa*, the power to read "at sight" in English, and in the case of French and German to know the language conversationally. In Latin the texts are Cæsar's Bellum Gallicum and Virgil's Æneid; in Greek, Xenophon's Anabasis and Homer's Iliad; in French and German the texts are those prescribed by the University of Toronto for junior and senior matriculation.

Mathematics.—In mathematics the course consists of advanced arithmetic, mensuration, algebra, six books of Euclid, and a moderate course in trigonometry.

Science.—In science the course is largely experimental. Every high school is equipped with a chemical and physical laboratory, and with all modern appliances for the study of chemistry, physics, botany, and zoölogy.

Commercial.—The course in bookkeeping and stenography is expected to qualify pupils for the work of banking houses, insurance companies, customhouses, and excise.

Physical Culture.—By the regulations of the department it is provided that drill and calisthenics shall be taught during the regular school hours, and in organized classes not less than half an hour per week to the pupils in the first three forms. The course in these exercises is the same as that prescribed in the military schools of the province. When the weather is not suitable, or where the pupils are physically incapable of taking this course, the principal may dispense with it. Every collegiate institute (by that is meant a high school of superior standing) is supplied with a gymnasium suitably furnished with mattresses, rings, ladders, and other appliances for gymnastic exercises, where pupils receive systematic instruction from a competent teacher. Outdoor sports of all kinds are encouraged, and many high schools have football teams and baseball clubs, by means of which ample physical exercise is obtained.

Qualifications of Teachers.—No person is eligible for appointment as principal of a high school (*a*) unless he is a graduate in arts of some university in the British dominions, (*b*) unless he passes the examination prescribed for the training of teachers in the Normal College; and (c) unless he has taught two years successfully as an assistant.

No teacher is eligible for appointment as an assistant teacher (a) who does not possess first-class literary standing, and (b) who has not passed the examinations prescribed by the Normal College.

The holidays in high schools are the same as those of public schools in cities, towns, and incorporated villages.

High schools are inspected by officers appointed by the Education Department, who report annually to the Minister of Education with regard to their standing, progress, equipment, and all matters covered by the regulations of the Education Department.

Upper Canada College.

Owing to the disputes arising over the sectarian character of King's College, Sir John Colborne, then Lieutenant-Governor, suspended the charter of the college, and established in 1829 a Royal grammar school in the city of Toronto, which has been known ever since as Upper Canada College. About sixty thousand acres of the land appropriated for grammar school and university purposes were set apart for its endowment.

As regards its organization, Upper Canada College was designed to be a residential school after the manner of the great public schools of England, such as Eton and Rugby. Its course of study was to lead up to university matriculation, and by means of the discipline and supervision exercised over its pupils in residence, it was intended to afford moral, intellectual, and physical training equal to the great schools after which it was modelled. For about forty years Upper Canada College supplied the best preliminary training available for a university career. In later years this work has been divided with the high schools. Upper Canada College differs from the high schools in the following respects :

1. It is a residential school, although a certain number of pupils are admitted as day pupils.

2. No preliminary examination is required for admission.

3. Its trustees are partly appointed by the Executive Government and partly by the alumni of the college.

4. Its courses of study and organization are not subject to the regulations imposed upon high schools.

5. It is not subject to the same inspection as high schools.

Notwithstanding these distinctions, Upper Canada College still prepares pupils for matriculation in arts, law, or medicine. Its special advantages are not, however, its courses of study, although these are equal to the best high school in the province, but in the discipline and training incident to residential schools, the freedom from distraction which residence of five or six years affords, the physical culture of the gymnasium and the playground, and the development of self-reliance and manliness arising from well-organized games and sports. These advantages, together with the broad and thorough literary training of the college, have made it a very important element in the educational equipment of the province for about sixty years.

As at present organized the trustees of the college recommend all appointments to the staff of the college, and make such regulations as, in their opinion, are necessary to its successful administration. Such appointments and regulations are subject to the approval of the Executive Government. The staff of the college consists of a principal who resides in the college, four assistants who also reside in the college, and as many day masters as the attendance of pupils renders necessary, including instructors in drill and gymnastics, music and stenography. For physical culture there are a gymnasium, skating rink, a running course with ample grounds for cricket, football, and tennis. The buildings now occupied by the college were erected in 1890 at a cost of over three hundred thousand dollars, and afford ample class-room accommodation for three hundred pupils with dormitories for one hundred and fifty boys. There are besides, a large assembly hall, and a well-equipped library and reading room. The fees for residence and tuition are $240 per annum; for tuition alone, $60 per annum.

CHAPTER VIII.

INSPECTION OF SCHOOLS AND RELIGIOUS INSTRUCTION.

THE Education Department is charged with the duty of inspecting the different classes of schools which constitute the school system of the province—viz., public schools, high schools, separate schools, model schools, and teachers' institutes. Normal schools are not made the subject of inspection, as they are immediately under the direction of the Minister of Education.

The inspectors of public schools in rural districts are appointed by County Councils; in urban districts, by the Board of Trustees; all other inspectors are appointed by the Education Department. As the jurisdiction of public-school inspectors is limited to one hundred and twenty schools, the larger counties are divided into two or more districts, each district being under a separate inspector. For high schools two inspectors are required; for separate schools, two; for model schools, one; and for teachers' institutes, one. Public-school inspectors are appointed during pleasure, and are liable to dismissal for misconduct or inefficiency by the Executive Government of the province or by the body by which they were appointed. They are paid at the rate of ten dollars for every school inspected, and, in addition, reasonable travelling expenses as the County Council may determine.

Qualifications of Inspectors.—The qualifications for a

public-school inspector are : (*a*) Five years' successful experience as a teacher, of which at least three years shall have been in a public school; and (*b*) a specialist's certificate obtained on a university examination, or a degree in arts from the University of Toronto with first-class graduation honours in one or more of the recognised departments of the university, or an equivalent standing in any other university of Ontario, with a certificate of having passed the final examination of the provincial School of Pedagogy, now called Normal College.

A high standard of literary qualification has been fixed by the department in order to secure the best men in the profession for inspection purposes. This is all the more important, as the inspector is a member of the Board of Examiners that determines the qualifications of pupils for admission to high schools and of candidates for teachers' third-class certificates. On account of their standing and experience, inspectors are also selected by the Minister of Education to assist in conducting the normal-school examinations, and in determining the teaching power of candidates for second-class certificates.

The qualifications of inspectors of separate schools are the same as those of inspectors for public schools. Inspectors of high schools are selected from the most experienced and successful high-school principals, and inspectors of model schools and teachers' institutes from those who have shown special aptitude for that kind of work.

Duties of Public-School Inspectors.—By the instructions of the department the public-school inspector is required to visit every school in his district twice during the year, and to spend at least half a day in the school at each visit. Where a school has several departments he is required to devote half a day to each department. If it is considered necessary in the interest of the school that he should extend his visit over a longer period or visit a school more than twice during the year, he is expected to do so. During his inspection he is required to make memoranda of the standing of each class and of the proficiency of the pupils in the various subjects of the public-school course of study. In order to satisfy himself as to the efficiency of the school, he is to examine the classes himself, either orally or by written work, so as to test thoroughly their attainments and to keep a record of the results of each examination. Where he finds any subject badly taught as to method, he is expected to illustrate by the teaching of a lesson in that subject how it should be taught for the benefit of the teacher and pupils. Notes are taken of the discipline of the school, and an estimate formed of the teacher's fitness for his position by studying his manner and methods in teaching such subjects as may be assigned to him for that purpose. Where the inspector finds defects in organization or in methods of instruction, he is required to point them out to the teacher at the close of his inspection, and at the same time to make a record of them for consideration at his next visit. With regard to the equipment of the school, he is to see (*a*) that the registers and class books are properly and neatly kept, and ascertain whether or not entries are made therein daily; (*b*) that the maps are suitable and well preserved; (*c*) that blackboards are in proper repair, and that crayons and brushes are fully supplied; (*d*) that the furniture is generally adequate; (*e*) that proper attention is paid to the heating and ventilation of the rooms; (*f*) that the fences and outhouses are in proper repair; (*g*) that the school library is properly cared for.

As soon as possible after his visit he reports to the trustees with regard to the standing of the school, the efficiency of the teachers, the equipment of the school, and any other matter which requires their attention. If he finds unauthorized text-books in the school, the equipment deficient, or the regulations of the department generally neglected, he is required to make a special report to the Minister of Education, who has power to withhold the Government grant from such school until the defects reported by the inspector are removed.

The public-school inspector is responsible, in a certain sense, for protecting the good name of the profession, and should he be aware that any teacher is guilty of immorality or has become so incompetent as to discredit the profession, he may suspend his certificate and call a meeting of the Board of Examiners of the county for the purpose of making a full inquiry into such complaints.

In addition to his duties as public-school inspector, he is required to visit the county model school of his district twice during the term, and to attend the meetings of the teachers' institutes and to take part in their proceedings. He takes charge of all local examinations conducted by the Education Department, makes up such statistical returns as are required by the department in regard to the enrollment of pupils, their classification, local expenditure for school purposes, etc. Though not appointed by the department, he is to all intents and purposes an officer of the department, and responsible for the proper enforcement of all regulations respecting public schools and for educating public opinion in respect to every question affecting the educational interests of the province. In many cases he is a judicial officer, as he decides upon disputes between trustees and teacher or acts as an arbitrator in the selection of school sites or in the adjustment of school boundaries. In the discharge of his duties it is assumed that he will act from the highest motives and so conduct himself as to enjoy the undoubted confidence of the public, irrespective of any private opinion which he may entertain, either on political or religious questions.

The duties of the separate-school inspectors are analogous in every respect to those of public-school inspectors, but, being appointed by the Education Department, they are not in any way under the control of County Councils.

High-School Inspection.—For the purpose of inspecting high schools the province is divided into two districts. Each high-school inspector is required to visit the schools of his district at least once a year. At the end of two years he exchanges districts with his colleague. He is guided in his inspection by the educational standard, prescribed for high schools, and it is his duty to see that these standards are maintained ; he has similar duties with regard to the inspection of high-school premises, the equipment of the high schools, etc., as public-school inspectors have with regard to public schools. He is also an officer of the department, and prepares the papers for entrance to high schools and such other examination papers of a professional character as the department may require from time to time.

Inspection of Model Schools.—The model-school inspector is required to visit all the model schools in the province at least once in two years, and to see that they are conducted according to the regulations of the department. It is his duty to examine the model-school students with regard to the methods of instruction practised in the model school, to see that the practice school attached is properly organized, and to give such advice to the principal of the model school and the teachers in training as he may consider necessary for their welfare.

Inspection of Teachers' Institutes.—The inspector of teachers' institutes is required to attend meetings of the teachers' institute and to discuss such matters affecting school organization and methods of teaching as the public-school inspector might suggest. He is expected to give addresses on subjects of a popular or pedagogical character which would tend to arouse greater interest in education, to correct misapprehensions as to the work of the teacher, or to excite a greater interest in literary or scientific study.

Under the democratic influences which have so rapidly developed in this century, it is sometimes feared that the educational interests of the people may become subservient to the aims and ambitions of the partisan and the political adventurer. It can not be said that in working out the school system of Ontario there is absolutely no political interference, that trustees are always elected because of fitness, and that teachers and inspectors are appointed purely on their merits. In the latter case, however, no matter to what political party the inspector belongs, the public is reasonably well protected against incompetence, if not against mediocrity, by the fact that no person is eligible to fill the position of inspector who does not possess certain fixed qualifications of a very substantial character, Any partisanship in the discharge of his duties would only invite criticism and imperil a position of great dignity and of comfortable emolument. The experience of twenty-five years shows that officers of this class fully realize the responsibilities of their position, and although several have retired of their own motion, only one, so far as known, has been dismissed because of his political partisanship.

In the appointment of teachers, similar conditions prevail. It probably can not be said that no trustee is uninfluenced in his choice by the political or denominational leanings of the applicant. It may, however, be said that appointments from political motives are exceptional, and that teachers who exercise the franchise as citizens do so without offensively interfering in political contests. Even in Parliament, legislation with regard to school matters is generally discussed upon its merits and independently of those political considerations which so largely influence the judgment and conduct of opposing political camps.

Religious Instruction.—In the early organization of the public schools of Ontario, no rules were laid down with regard to the religious instruction of the pupils. The absence of any central authority for the direction of the teacher or for the adequate inspection of schools permitted a large measure of freedom in this matter as well as in all other matters pertaining to public-school education. It was not until the organization of a Department of Education under a chief superintendent, in 1846, that directions were given to the teachers either with regard to morals or religion.

In the regulations of the department, issued in 1850, the teacher was enjoined "to pay the strictest attention to the morals and general conduct of his pupils, and to omit no opportunity of inculcating the principles of truth and honesty; the duties of respect to superiors, and obedience to all persons placed in authority over them; to evince a regard for the improvement and general welfare of his pupils; to treat them with kindness combined with firmness; and to aim at governing them by their affections and reason, rather than by harshness and severity; to cultivate kindly and affectionate feelings among his pupils; to discountenance quarrelling, cruelty to animals, and every approach to vice." These, however, are moral obligations necessarily involved in the relation of teacher and pupil, and must be enforced in any school, even where the doctrines of Christianity are not the recognised standards of faith and practice.

In the regulations adopted on the 5th day of August, 1850, the Education Department made its first advance toward direct religious instruction, and " with a view to secure the Divine blessing, and to impress upon the pupils the importance of religious duties and their entire dependence upon their Maker," the department recommended that " the daily exercises of each public school be opened and closed by reading a portion of Scripture, and by prayer. The Lord's Prayer alone, or the forms of prayer approved by the department, may be used, or any other prayer preferred by the trustees and master of each school. But the Lord's Prayer shall form part of the opening exercise, and the Ten Commandments shall be taught to all the pupils, and be repeated at least once a week; but no pupil shall be compelled to be present at these exercises against the wish of his parent or guardian, expressed in writing to the master of the school."

It will be observed that the religious exercises here enjoined are a matter of voluntary arrangement. The School Act of 1843 provided that " no child shall be required to read or study in or from any religious book, or to join in any exercise of devotion or religion, which shall be objected to by his or her parents or guardians: provided always that, within this limitation, pupils shall be allowed to receive such religious instruction as their parents or guardians shall desire, according to the general regulations which shall be provided according to law."

In these regulations religious instruction, at least so far as the reading of the Scriptures and devotional exercises were concerned, was given in the majority of schools of the province with very satisfactory results. To improve and systematize the religious instruction of pupils, select Scripture readings were authorized, and a text-book was prepared by the chief superintendent, entitled Lessons on the Truths of Christianity for the use of public schools.

The importance of religious instruction, or at least of the recognition of Christianity and its teachings, as part of the educational outfit of the pupil, has been recognised by the Education Department ever since the school system was regularly organized, and where a proper regard is paid to the conscientious scruples of parents and guardians there is no reason why that recognition should not find expression in an authoritative way. To make it obligatory for teachers to conduct religious instruction of any kind might be to impose a burden upon their conscience, which no state authority has a right to impose. To authorize them, if they were so inclined, to explain the Scriptures might lead to the propagation of dogmas incompatible with their usefulness as teachers, and involving departmental responsibility inconsistent with a popular system of education. The Education Department, however, impressed with the necessity of giving at least a legal sanction to the teachings of Christianity in all the public schools of the province, authorized in 1885 a series of Scripture readings and forms of prayer, the use of which was obligatory in all public and high schools. If the teacher had any conscientious scruples against the reading of the Scriptures and the opening and closing of the school by prayer, he was to be considered as discharged from the performance of this duty. Parents or guardians had the right to withdraw their children from such religious exercises at their discretion.

Where religious instruction of a more formal character was desired, the privilege was allowed the clergy of any denomination or their authorized representative to give religious instruction to pupils of their own church in each schoolhouse at least once a week after the hour of closing in the afternoon. Trustees have also the power of reducing the hours of regular study in order to afford facilities for religious instruction.

The statistics of the department show that the regulations with regard to religious instruction are generally observed. In 1894 the Scriptures were read in ninety per cent of the rural schools of the province, and the devotional exercises sanctioned by the department were used in ninety-three per cent of the schools. In every urban school except two the Scriptures were read daily, and every urban school without exception was opened and closed with devotional exercises. In three hundred and sixty-nine of the rural schools religious instruction was given by clergymen after school hours, and frequent visits were paid to many other schools as an expression of their sympathy with the work of the teacher.

In separate schools, whether Protestant or Catholic, as already intimated, the Education Department assumes no responsibility with regard to religious instruction.

Departmental Regulations.—From the interest which attaches to this question, the regulations of the department are given in detail, and are as follows:

1. Every public and high school shall be opened with the Lord's Prayer, and closed with the reading of the

Scriptures and the Lord's Prayer, or the prayer authorized by the Department of Education.

2. The Scriptures shall be read daily and systematically without comment or explanation, and the portions used may be taken from the book of selections adopted by the department for that purpose, or from the Bible, as the trustees by resolution may direct.

3. Trustees may also order the reading of the Bible or the authorized Scripture selections by both pupils and teachers at the opening and closing of the school, and the repeating of the Ten Commandments at least once a week.

4. No pupil shall be required to take part in any religious exercise objected to by his parents or guardians, and in order to the observance of this regulation, the teacher, before commencing a religious exercise, is to allow a short interval to elapse, during which the children of Roman Catholics, and of others who have signified their objection, may retire.

5. If in virtue of the right to be absent from the religious exercises, any pupil does not enter the schoolroom till fifteen minutes after the proper time for opening the school in the forenoon, such absence shall not be treated as an offence against the rules of the school.

6. When a teacher claims to have conscientious scruples in regard to opening or closing the school as herein prescribed, he shall notify the trustees to that effect in writing; and it shall be the duty of the trustees to make such provision in the premises as they may deem expedient.

7. The clergy of any denomination, or their authorized representatives, shall have the right to give religious instruction to the pupils of their own church, in each school-

house, at least once a week, after the hour of closing the school in the afternoon; and if the clergy of more than one denomination apply to give religious instruction in the same schoolhouse, the Board of Trustees shall decide on what day of the week the schoolhouse shall be at the disposal of the clergymen of each denomination at the time above stated. But it shall be lawful for the Board of Trustees and clergymen of any denomination to agree upon any hour of the day at which a clergyman, or his authorized representative, may give religious instruction to the pupils of his own church, provided it be not during the regular hours of the school. Emblems of a denominational character shall not be exhibited in a public school during regular school hours.

CHAPTER IX.

DENOMINATIONAL SCHOOLS.

UNDER the Act of 1816 the trustees of common schools were the sole judges of the qualifications of teachers. They were also authorized to make rules and regulations for the good government of the schools with respect to the teachers and pupils and to determine what text-books should be used, subject to the approval of the Boards of Education for the district.

The Boards of Trustees, therefore, practically determined not only who should conduct their schools, but the text-books to be used and the course of study which should be observed both by teachers and pupils. In localities where the majority were Protestants, Protestant teachers were employed; and owing partly to the scarcity of text-books and partly to the education which the early settlers had received in the schools of Great Britain and Ireland, the Bible was almost invariably used as a text-book in reading. Where the majority were Roman Catholics they had the right to use the powers which the school act conferred upon them, and to direct both the secular and religious training of their children at the common school.

Act of 1841.—On the union of Upper and Lower Canada (Ontario and Quebec) in 1841, the establishment of common schools and their improvement was one of the questions that early engaged the attention of the Legislature. In his address at the opening of Parliament, Lord Sydenham, the first Governor-General, used the following language:

"A due provision for the education of the people is one of the first duties of the state, and, in this province especially, the want of it is grievously felt. The establishment of an efficient system, by which the blessings of instruction may be placed within the reach of all, is a work of difficulty, but its overwhelming importance demands that it should be undertaken. I recommend the consideration of that subject to your best attention, and I shall be most anxious to afford you, in your labours, all the co-operation in my power. If it should be found impossible so to reconcile conflicting opinions as to obtain a measure which may meet the approbation of all, I trust that at least steps may be taken by which an advance to a more perfect system may be made, and the difficulty under which the people of this province now labour may be greatly diminished, subject to such improvements hereafter as time and experience may point out."

In response to this request of the Governor-General, Solicitor-General Day, afterward the Hon. Mr. Justice Day, introduced a bill for the improvement of the school system of the province. Petitions were presented to the House urging the Legislature duly to recognise religious instruction as an essential part of the common-school education. As an illustration of the urgency of this demand, the following quotation from a petition signed by clergymen and members of the Church of England may be taken : " Wherefore your petitioners humbly pray that not only may the Bible be recognised as the class book to be universally taught in all public schools and seminaries throughout the province in which Protestants shall receive their education, but that it may be put into the hands of all such scholars in its full unabridged state, and that no part of it may be withheld from them." The Moderator of the Presbyterian Church of Canada, on behalf of the Presbyterians, prayed " that an enactment be made for the use of the Bible in all the schools of the province." The Roman Catholic bishops of Quebec prayed " that in framing any school act for the improvement of education, care should be taken that it shall contain no enactment that can prejudice the interest of her Majesty's Roman Catholic subjects." Of the forty-two petitions presented, thirty-nine were from Protestants, and called for the use of the Bible in the schools.

The bill submitted by Mr. Daly and the petitions presented with regard to education were referred to a select committee of twenty-two—eight from Ontario and fourteen from Quebec.* As a result of the deliberations of the committee, a bill was reported which received the royal assent on the 18th day of September, 1841, and which contained the following clause : " Provided always, and be it enacted, that whenever any number of the inhabitants of any township or parish, professing a religious faith different from that of the majority of the inhabitants of such township or parish, shall dissent from the regulations, arrangements, or proceedings of the common-school commissioners, with reference to any common school in such township or parish, it shall be lawful for the inhabitants so dissenting, collectively, to signify such dissent in writ-

---

* The Ontario members were Messrs. John S. Cartwright, Malcolm Cameron, Duncombe, Merritt, Park, Thorburn, Francis Hincks, and John Prince. The Quebec members were Messrs. Neilson, Simpson, Moffat, Quesnel, Allwin, Christie, Morin, Child, Parent, Robertson, Holmes, Foster, Berthelot, and Viger.

ing to the clerk of the district council, with the name or names of one or more persons elected by them as their trustee or trustees, for the purposes of this act; and the said district clerk shall forthwith furnish a certified copy thereof to the district treasurer; and it shall be lawful for such dissenting inhabitants, by and through such trustee or trustees, who for that purpose shall hold and exercise all rights, powers, and authorities, and be subject to the obligations and liabilities hereinbefore assigned to and imposed upon the common-school commissioners, to establish and maintain one or more common schools in the manner, and subject to the visitation, conditions, rules, and obligations, in this act provided with reference to other common schools, and to receive from the district treasurer their due proportion, according to their number, of the moneys appropriated by law, and raised by assessment for the support of common schools, in the school district or districts in which the said inhabitants reside, in the same manner as if the common schools so to be established and maintained under such trustee or trustees were established and maintained under the said common-school commissioners, such moneys to be paid by the district treasurer upon the warrant of the said trustee and trustees."

By section 16 of the same act, provision was made for the appointment of Boards of Examiners for each city or town, to be composed of not less than six nor more than fourteen persons, half of whom should be Protestants and the other half Roman Catholics. The mayor of the city or town was *ex officio* chairman of the board. The Catholic section was given full jurisdiction over all the schools attended by Roman Catholics, and had a right to appoint its own chairman. The Protestant section had similar powers with regard to schools attended by Protestant children. In the case of mixed schools, the board, as a whole, exercised undivided jurisdiction. This board, or either section of it, had power to examine candidates for teachers' certificates, to select the text-books for pupils, and to make rules and regulations for the government of the schools of their section.

By section 4 of the act it was provided that no person should be appointed a teacher in any school who was not a subject of her Majesty either by birth or by naturalization, and who had not passed an examination as to his ability as a teacher before the proper authorities, unless such person belonged to the order known as *Les Frères de la Doctrine Chrétienne*.

This is the first recognition of denominational schools by act of Parliament in the history of Ontario, containing in these sections all the characteristics of the present Separate-School Act of the province, viz.:

1. The right of Roman Catholics to establish separate schools for their own children.

2. The right to appoint teachers of their own faith.

3. The right to public moneys for the maintenance of their own schools.

4. The right of members of a religious order to be recognised teachers without examination.

Act of 1843.—Owing to the dissimilar educational interests of the two provinces the Act of 1841 was repealed, and in 1843 separate acts were passed for each province. In the act passed for Ontario, the principle of the Act of 1841 with regard to denominational schools was retained, but in a modified form.

1. It was provided that no separate school could be established for Roman Catholics unless the teacher of the common school was a Protestant, and no separate school

DENOMINATIONAL SCHOOLS. 145

could be established for Protestants unless the teacher was a Roman Catholic.

2. Application for a separate school must be signed by ten or more resident freeholders or householders of the school section or of the city or town in which it was proposed to establish a separate school, and approved by the council or local superintendent.

3. On such approval being given, the separate school was entitled to receive its share of public grants according to the number of children in attendance. Separate schools, however, were to be subject to the same inspection as common schools, and the course of study to the approval of the school superintendent of the district.

In 1850 it was provided that no separate school should be established for Protestants or Roman Catholics except on the petition of twelve heads of families, instead of the petition of ten householders, as under the previous acts. Public aid was to be given upon the average attendance at separate schools as compared with the average attendance at common schools of the district. No change was made with regard to other provisions of previous acts of Parliament.

Although Protestants and Catholics were thus allowed the privilege of establishing separate schools for the children of their own faith, and although they shared in the grant made by the Legislature for the maintenance of common schools, they were nevertheless liable for all assessments for the maintenance of common schools which the municipality might impose. The effect of this provision of the law was that they were doubly burdened: first, for the necessary school accommodation for their own children; and, second, for the maintenance of the common or mixed schools, from which they received no

11

direct benefit. The Roman Catholics claimed that as the principle of separate schools at which they could educate their own children practically in their own way was conceded, and as they were permitted to share in the grants made by the Government to common schools, they should not be subject to this double burden.

Act of 1852.—As a consequence of this demand, the Common-School Act of Ontario was amended in 1852, by which separate schools were allowed the following privileges:

1. Where the supporters of a separate school raised by subscription an amount equal to the assessment imposed by the trustees of the common schools for common-school purposes, then such separate-school supporters should be exempted from all rates for the support of the common school.

2. The Government grant payable to separate schools was to be in proportion to the average attendance of children at separate schools, as compared with the attendance of common schools in the same municipality.

3. So soon as the supporters of separate schools ceased to subscribe an amount equal to the sum for which they would be liable for common-school purposes, then they became liable for common-school rates.

4. A certificate of qualification signed by a majority of the trustees of a separate school was sufficient qualification for a separate-school teacher. Under the previous act separate-school teachers were examined by the district Board of Examiners.

5. Separate-school trustees were constituted corporations with power to impose school rates upon persons sending children to or subscribing toward the support of separate schools, and they were invested with the same

DENOMINATIONAL SCHOOLS. 147

power to collect school rates as were enjoyed by the trustees of common schools. This power they did not possess under previous acts.

6. The supporters of separate schools were not allowed to vote at the election of trustees for common schools.

Act of 1855.—In 1855 the question of separate schools was again before the Legislative Assembly, and a short bill passed repealing all previous legislation with regard to separate schools, but re-enacting in a different form nearly all the privileges which the Legislature had conferred upon them in previous years.

As the question had now entered the political arena, and had been taken up with that intensity which characterizes the contests of political parties, it became quite apparent that any settlement that did not meet the reasonable expectation of the Roman Catholics was but to prolong the struggle and to foster antagonisms which might prove injurious to the future of the whole country. Numerically, Roman Catholics and Protestants were about equal in population. The representatives from the Province of Quebec alleged that they were justified in supporting separate schools for the Catholics of Ontario, because of the liberal concessions they had made to the Protestant minority of their province. Parliament had by repeated legislation acknowledged the principle of separate schools; then why should Parliament, they asked, refuse such legislation as would give those for whom separate schools were intended greater control over them?

As a result of this agitation the election of members of Parliament was largely determined by their attitude with respect to separate schools. It was not, however, until 1863 that a measure was approved by the Legislature which practically placed the separate schools in the position they now occupy, and which has in a large measure relieved the question of that acuteness, at all events, as a political issue, which characterized it for the previous twenty years.

Act of 1863.—The bill of 1863 was introduced by Mr. R. W. Scott, member for the city of Ottawa, and now a member of the Senate of Canada. This bill was supported by twenty-two members from Ontario and by fifty-four from the Province of Quebec; of those who voted against it, thirty were from Ontario and only one from the Province of Quebec. Although amended in some respects by recent legislation, no material change has been made in any of its main features. And so separate schools for Roman Catholics and Protestants as they at present exist under the public-school system of the Province of Ontario may now be considered.

Organization of Roman Catholic Separate Schools.— Any number of persons, not less than five being heads of families, and householders or freeholders, resident within any school section of any township, incorporated village, or town, or within any ward of any city or town, being Roman Catholics, may convene a public meeting of persons desiring to establish a separate school for Roman Catholics for the purpose of electing three trustees for the management of such school. Notice of this meeting must be given to the reeve or head of the municipality or to the chairman of the School Board, and from the day of the delivery and receipt of such notice the persons elected at this meeting become a corporation for separate-school purposes.

In rural schools three trustees constitute a corporation. In urban schools two trustees are elected for each ward into which the municipality is divided, the same as in the case of public schools. Any person being a British subject, twenty-one years of age, is eligible for election as a trustee, and any person twenty-one years of age who is a separate-school supporter has a right to vote for a separate-school trustee. Elections for separate-school trustees are held at the same time as elections for public-school trustees, and proceedings at such elections are in every respect similar. Where the Board of Trustees asks the election to be by ballot in cities, towns, or incorporated villages, the elections are so held; but instead of being conducted by municipal officers, as in the case of public-school elections, they are conducted by officers appointed by the separate-school board.

Who are Separate-School Supporters.—Any person who desires to become legally recognised as a separate-school supporter is required to give notice in writing to the clerk of the municipality that he is a Roman Catholic, and the supporter of a separate school situated in the municipality or in a municipality contiguous to the one in which he resides. Such notice exempts the person giving the same from the payment of all rates imposed for the support of public schools or for public-school libraries, or for the purchase of land for a school site, or for the erection of buildings for public-school purposes within the municipality or school section in which he resides, so long as such person continues a supporter of a separate school. It is not necessary that this notice shall be renewed annually.

While this notice relieves the person from all future liability for the maintenance of public schools, it does not, however, relieve him from any obligations that may have been incurred by the public-school trustees, such as the payment of debentures for school buildings while he was a public-school supporter. As it would be impossible for municipal councils to divide a municipality into public and separate-school sections, owing to the fact that Protestants and Roman Catholics are distributed generally throughout the municipality, the law provides that any person within three miles in a direct line of the site of the separate school, who gives the notice required by law, shall be deemed a separate-school supporter. The occupant or tenant of any land within the three-mile limit, if a Catholic, has the right to declare himself a separate-school supporter and to require that any tax chargeable on such land shall go for separate-school purposes. This right he enjoys even if the land is owned by a Protestant. Conversely, where the tenant is a Protestant and the owner a Catholic, the Protestant will be regarded as a public-school supporter. Although Protestants may, if they choose, send their children to a separate school, they can not claim exemption from public-school rates on that account.

Joint-stock companies may under certain conditions require that that portion of the joint-stock property owned by Roman Catholics, or their relative interest in the property, shall be assessed for separate-school purposes. The policy of the law is to allow Roman Catholics the privilege, where they have formed a separate school, of appropriating without any reservation, except as to previous obligations, all their property for the maintenance of their own schools.

If a Roman Catholic desires to withdraw his support from a separate school, he may do so on giving notice in writing to the clerk of the municipality, and in that case he is no longer liable for separate-school rates, but he remains liable for any debts incurred by the trustees of the separate school during the time he was rated as a supporter of it. Roman Catholics are as free to support a public school as a separate school, and, as a matter of fact, some of them do support the public school even where they are in reach of a separate school, although this is the exception and not the rule.

Separate Schools, how supported.—Separate schools are supported (*a*) by a grant from the provincial treasury, paid upon the basis of average attendance, subject to precisely the same conditions as the grant paid to public schools; (*b*) by a rate levied by the trustees upon the taxable property of the supporters of the school. This rate the trustees collect by officers of their own appointment or through the collector of the municipality, as they prefer; (*c*) by fees from the pupils attending separate schools.

By law, separate schools are not free, as the term is understood when applied to public schools, although as a matter of practice fees are not charged by any Board of Trustees in the province.

Separate-School Teachers.—There are two classes of teachers employed in separate schools: one class known as lay teachers, who are subject to the same examinations and receive their certificate of qualification in the same way as public-school teachers; the other class known as religious teachers, who are not, under the Separate-School Act, subject to any examination whatsoever. Of those employed in separate schools in 1894, 323 were lay teachers and 391 teachers belonging to some religious order.

It does not follow, however, because religious teachers are not subject to an examination, that they are either deficient in regard to literary qualifications or exempt from the control of the department. Should any teacher, whether lay or religious, be regarded as deficient, either as to his power of maintaining order or of advancing the efficiency of his pupils, it is within the province of the Education Department to withhold the school grant in such cases, and the trustees would be obliged to replace such teacher by some person who would discharge the duties satisfactorily to the department. Teachers of separate schools are under the same regulations with regard to their duties and privileges as the teachers of public schools. Complaints between teachers and trustees are settled either by the Minister of Education or before a county judge.

Courses of Study—Text-Books and Inspection.—The courses of study in separate schools are similar to those laid down by the regulations of the Education Department for public schools. With regard to text-books, a greater liberty of choice is permitted than in public schools. In the majority of separate schools public-school text-books are used, except in reading and history.

The separate schools are inspected by officers appointed by the Education Department. These officers possess the same qualifications as public-school inspectors; they conduct the inspection in a similar way, and report annually to the trustees of the school and to the Minister of Education as to the efficiency and standing of each school.

With regard to the religious instruction which constitutes an essential feature of separate schools, the department lays down no regulations and exercises no jurisdiction, nor does it fix any limit as to the time to be devoted to this purpose. All that is required in order to the payment of the school grant is that the efficiency of the school and the standing of the pupils are sufficiently meritorious, having regard to the attainments of pupils of the same age in the public schools. So far as departmental control is concerned, the Minister of Education stands in precisely the same relation to the separate schools as he does to any other branch of the school system, and no authority, lay or clerical, has a right to interfere with him in the legal discharge of his duties.

Protestant Separate Schools.—Side by side with the recognition of the privileges granted to Roman Catholics for the establishment of separate schools for the children of their own faith was recognised the principle of separate schools for the children of Protestants. Such schools are organized in the same way as Roman Catholic schools, with these exceptions:

1. Protestant separate schools can not be established unless the teacher is a Roman Catholic.

2. In order to be entitled to a grant by the Legislature, the supporters of Protestant separate schools must subscribe annually a sum equal to the amount which the supporters thereof would be rated in order to obtain the Government grant if such Protestant separate school did not exist.

3. Protestant separate-school supporters may withdraw by ceasing to subscribe for the support of a separate school or by sending their children to a public school.

Protestant separate schools are established only where a few Protestant families have settled in a school section controlled by Roman Catholics. So rarely is that control exercised in a manner distasteful to Protestants, that only ten separate Protestant schools exist in the whole province.

The qualifications of teachers in Protestant separate schools, the text-books used, and the supervision exercised over them are identical with that exercised in the case of public schools.

Coloured Separate Schools.—In a few localities in the province, owing to the existence of large settlements of coloured people, separate schools are permitted, at which the children of coloured people attend. These schools are organized, conducted, and inspected the same as Protestant separate schools.

It must be observed here that while under the school system of Ontario separate schools are allowed, there is no cleavage of a denominational character beyond the elementary or public school. In high schools, as well as in the university, no religious distinction of any kind is recognised either as to pupils, teachers, or courses of study. Should pupils, however, desire to absent themselves from the religious exercises of the high school or the devotional exercises of the university, they are at liberty to do so, and are not amenable to any discipline because of such action.

It may be said that separate schools are necessarily less efficient than public schools. This depends entirely upon the vigilance of the Education Department, and the thoroughness with which the work of inspection is conducted. Separate schools have no immunities under the school system of Ontario by which the standards of elementary education can be lowered or the intellectual improvement of the children attending them impaired. The whole question is one of administration, and the policy which produces an efficient public-school system will, if honestly administered, produce the same results in the separate schools.

Control of the Dominion Government over Separate Schools.—Under the British North America Act, power has been taken to pass legislation with regard to separate schools where, in the opinion of the Dominion Parliament, injustice has been done to the minority. For instance, if it should appear that the Protestant minority in Quebec, or the Roman Catholic minority in Ontario, or in any other province, were deprived of any right or privilege which they had by law at the time of the federation of the British provinces in 1867, it is held that the Dominion Parliament could pass remedial legislation restoring to the minority, in such cases, the privileges of which they were deprived by the Provincial Legislatures. In 1890 the Legislature of Manitoba repealed all previous legislation which had been passed for the establishment of separate schools in that province, substituting therefor a system of public schools for the province without any distinction as to denomination or creed. Considerable litigation arose out of this action of the Manitoba Legislature, the result of which has been that the Dominion Government considers itself called upon to interfere on behalf of the Roman Catholics of Manitoba, with a view to the re-establishment of separate schools in that province.

CHAPTER X.

SCHOOL LIBRARIES, PUBLIC LIBRARIES, AND TEXT-BOOKS.

IN the School Act of 1850 authority was given the Chief Superintendent of Education "to employ all lawful means in his power to promote the establishment of school libraries for general reading in the several townships, cities, towns, and incorporated villages of the province."

In order to assist in the establishment of such libraries, the Legislature voted the sum of $12,000, and authorized the chief superintendent to apportion the same, subject to the regulations of the Education Department. In 1853 the Education Department sanctioned the expenditure of this money for the establishment of libraries in school sections and in townships as the local authorities might see fit. Township councils were authorized to keep the library in some central place in the township, or to divide it into as many parts as there were school sections in the township. When the library was divided into sections the trustees were required—at regular periods of not more than a year—to see that the portion allotted to them was transferred to another school section, and in this way the books were removed from one section to another in rotation. The Education Department also authorized the preparation of a catalogue, and the choice of books was

SCHOOL LIBRARIES AND PUBLIC LIBRARIES. 157

limited to the list so prepared. The Government grant to libraries was equal to the amount raised by the locality. In order to guard against the circulation of unsuitable books, the Education Department established a book depository and imported books from the foreign market for the use of section and township libraries. The book trade, however, regarded such a depository as a competitor with the legitimate book-selling business, and in 1881 the depository was abolished and libraries supplied through the ordinary channels of trade.

Although the effort to establish school libraries was not as satisfactory as could be desired, they proved of great advantage to some of the more remote parts of the province. In the twenty-nine years during which the Education Depository existed 298,743 volumes were sent out to school sections and township libraries, valued at $178,516. School libraries ceased to exist with the withdrawal of the grant. Their place has, however, been more than filled by the establishment of public libraries in all parts of the province.

Public libraries were first known under the term " Mechanics' Institutes." The first institute in Ontario was opened in Toronto in 1835, and received a grant from the Legislature of $400 for the purchase of books and philosophical instruments. In the same year a library was opened at Kingston, and in 1842 another at London, all of which received aid from the provincial treasury.

In 1868 provision was made for the establishment of evening classes in connection with public libraries, and for the founding of a reference library to consist of books on architecture, engineering and building, manufactures and industrial art, agriculture and horticulture, technical chemistry and experimental philosophy. The Government grant paid to each public library was to be proportioned to the amount of money expended by the local board on books of a scientific character. In 1872 public libraries were subjected to the supervision of the Inspectors of Public Schools who were to report with regard to them to the Education Department.

Notwithstanding the anxiety of the Legislature to promote the establishment of public libraries, the progress made was not satisfactory. The great difficulty in maintaining them as the law then existed was the want of local support. The directors were dependent entirely upon voluntary subscriptions and the small grant made by the Government. After paying the rent of rooms and other expenses of maintenance the sum available for books was necessarily very small, and it was difficult for the board to find the means of supplying libraries with fresh and attractive literature.

Free Libraries. — In 1882 an act called the Public Libraries Act was passed, which authorized the municipal council of any city, town, or incorporated village on the petition of a certain number of electors, to submit a by-law to the votes of the ratepayers for the establishment of a free public library. A board of management was constituted under this act, consisting of the mayor of the city or town or the reeve of the village, three other persons to be appointed by the council of the municipality, three by the Public School Board, and two by the Separate-School Board of the city or town in which the library was to be located. This board was to have the power of purchasing a site and erecting suitable buildings for a library and reading room. It was also to have the general management, regulation, and control of the library and reading room, with power to make regulations for the purchase, circula-

SCHOOL LIBRARIES AND PUBLIC LIBRARIES. 159

tion, and distribution of books and papers. As a corporation the board had the right of fixing its own meetings and carrying on its business independent of all municipal control. The money required for buildings and equipment was raised by the debentures of the municipality. The annual expenditure of the board (not including buildings) was limited to the amount that would be produced by a rate of half a mill on the dollar on the real and personal property of the municipality. In the case of cities with a population over 100,000 this amount was not to exceed one quarter of a mill on the dollar. The library and reading room were to be free to all residents of the municipality.

The first free public library established under this act was opened in Toronto in 1884. The expenditure of the board on buildings and books has already amounted to over $200,000. In addition to a circulating library, the board of management has established a very valuable reference library of over 30,000 volumes.

Subsequently free public libraries have been opened and maintained by the municipalities under the Act of 1882 in eight cities and in four of the large towns of the province, with assets estimated at $330,000, containing 165,000 volumes, and an aggregate circulation for the year of over 1,500,000 volumes. The appropriation of the Government for each library and reading room is $250 in cities and $200 in towns. The annual expenditure for library purposes by the province (including local and Government grants) in 1895 was over $150,000.

Minor Free Libraries.—The greatest obstacle to the general establishment of free libraries is the cost of suitable buildings and premises. In small municipalities it has been found, however, that while the people may not be willing to incur the larger expenditure necessary for a library building, they are not unwilling to contribute annually a moderate sum for the purchase of books and for contingent expenses. Accordingly, in 1895 the Public Libraries Act was amended, authorizing municipal councils to appoint a board of management for library purposes, even where a by-law had not been passed for the erection of buildings. In such cases the income of the board depends upon the bounty of the municipality from year to year, the amount of money received from voluntary subscriptions, and the appropriations made by the Government from the provincial treasury. Already fifteen free libraries have been established under this act, in addition to those for whose accommodation the municipalities have made provision under the Act of 1882.

But there were still places of a more isolated character, in which it was desirable to provide facilities for the circulation of good literature, and where no aid was likely to be received from municipal authorities. In such cases it was provided that ten persons could constitute themselves a corporation, under the Public Libraries Act, with the right to appoint a board of management for library purposes. In this way a public library may be established in any village, however small, but no grant is paid by the Government unless the board of management is able to show that one hundred persons over twelve years of age, fifty of whom shall be over twenty-one years of age, have subscribed themselves as members—membership in this case meaning that the persons so subscribing intend to avail themselves of the privileges of a library. Such boards are dependent entirely upon voluntary contributions and upon the Government grant amounting to $100.

This class of library is simply a modification of the Mechanics' Institute Act of 1851, and has been of greater service to the public than any other class of library aided by the Government. In 1895 there were 318 libraries of this class in the country, having a total circulation of 644,000 volumes.

Government Grant.—Public libraries are aided by the Legislature, subject to the regulations of the Education Department, on the following conditions:

1. The sum of one dollar is allowed for every dollar invested annually by the board of management in the purchase of books, but so as not to exceed $200 in the case of cities, $150 in the case of towns, and in all other cases $100.

2. A further sum of one dollar is allowed each public library for every dollar expended on newspapers and magazines for the purpose of a reading room, but so as not to exceed $50 for each reading room.

Where public libraries establish evening classes, a sum of three dollars is allowed for every pupil, providing the class is composed of twenty-five or under, with an additional allowance of one dollar per pupil for all over twenty-five, but so as not to exceed the sum of $100 for evening classes to each board.

Regulations respecting Public Libraries.—Public libraries, for which the municipality has not provided the necessary buildings, are subject to the following regulations:

1. The building selected for the accommodation of the public library and reading room shall be conveniently situated and shall be easy of access to the public. The words "Public Library" shall be painted on or over the outside door of the building or in some other conspicuous place, in letters not less than four inches in length and three inches in width.

2. The rooms shall be properly warmed and lighted,

and shall be furnished with suitable racks and files for papers and with seating accommodation for at least ten persons. The reading room shall contain on separate files at least two daily newspapers, five weeklies, and three standard monthly magazines. The Government grant shall be based on the amount expended by the board of management.

3. The library and reading room shall be open to the public for the delivery and exchange of books and the perusal of papers and magazines at least three times every week, on such days and at such hours as the board of management may direct, subject to the approval of the Education Department.

4. All books shall be properly stamped, labelled, shelved, and kept in good order, and shall be insured for the total amount contributed by the Government during the last ten preceding years.

5. The Government grant shall be paid for books bought within the official year, on the declaration of the president and librarian that the books have been received, labelled, and shelved. A receipted invoice of the books purchased for the library and a certified account of the expenditure on supplies for the reading room should accompany the declaration. Only twenty per cent of the Government grant for books will be allowed for expenditure on fiction.

6. All books, registers, and account books and invoices used in connection with any public library, reading room, evening classes, or art school shall be open at all convenient hours to such inspection as the Minister of Education may direct.

Evening Classes and Art Schools.—By a reference to the chapter on the Courses of Study in Public and High

SCHOOL LIBRARIES AND PUBLIC LIBRARIES. 163

Schools it will be seen that elementary drawing is one of the obligatory subjects of study. In order to promote the further study of this subject, particularly with a view to mechanical and industrial purposes, the board of management having charge of a public library is authorized to establish evening classes in drawing, such classes to take the following courses:

1. Primary drawing, viz., free-hand drawing from flat examples, practical geometry, linear perspective, model drawing, and object or memory drawing. 2. Advance drawing, viz., shading from flat examples, outline drawing from the round, shading from the round, drawing from flowers and objects of natural history, and industrial design. 3. Mechanical drawing, viz., projection and descriptive geometry, machine drawing, building construction, architectural design, and advanced perspective. 4. Industrial art course, viz., modelling in clay, wood carving, engraving, lithography, painting on china.

Classes may also be formed in botany, chemistry, or physical science, the course in any of these subjects being the same as that prescribed in forms I, II, and III of high schools.

In order to be entitled to Government aid, the board of management must provide ample accommodation and equipment for teaching the subjects in the courses prescribed, and must be supplied with a staff of teachers satisfactory to the Education Department.

Examinations are conducted annually by the Education Department, and certificates, medals, and other distinctions awarded on the basis of such examinations. In 1895 there were forty-two evening classes established in connection with public libraries, with an attendance of 966 pupils.

Text-Books.

Since the appointment of a chief superintendent in 1846, the Education Department has had authority to regulate the use of text-books in public schools. If unauthorized text-books are used, the Government grant may be withheld, and any teacher who negligently or wilfully substitutes any unauthorized books for the authorized text-books in actual use in the same subjects in his school is liable, on conviction before a magistrate, to a penalty not exceeding ten dollars. When, in the opinion of the department, a text-book in actual use has to be changed, notice is given that a new text-book in the subject is available, but no new text-book can be introduced except at the beginning of a school term.

The policy of the Education Department with regard to text-books may be briefly summed up as follows:

1. That so far as practicable there shall be but one text-book in each subject in the course of study. So long as pupils are required to purchase their own text-books, it is considered undesirable that they should be put to the expense of providing a new set in case of their removal from one part of the province to another. Besides, as the courses of study are graded with reference to the authorized text-books both as a guide to the teacher and the inspector, a variety of books would render proper classification impossible. There may be some disadvantage to the pupils in limiting their reading to one series of readers, as facility in vocal expression is obtained largely from practice over a wider field than a single text-book affords. The abundance and cheapness, however, of literature of all kinds for children, and the general distribution of public libraries, have removed this objection, and an in-

SCHOOL LIBRARIES AND PUBLIC LIBRARIES. 165

telligent teacher need have no difficulty in inciting his pupils to read for themselves far more extensively than could be done from the number of text-books in reading used in any school.

2. That all text-books of doubtful merit shall be excluded from the public schools. Where trustees are allowed to determine the text-books to be used, they are not infrequently imposed upon by publishers who are seeking a market for their goods. As trustees have no special qualifications for judging whether a text-book is properly graded or not, or whether the subject of which it treats is logically developed, to allow them to select text-books for the use of schools would be to confer upon them a power, whether honestly exercised or not, which might injuriously affect the mental development of pupils. Few persons possess that knowledge of a subject and of the mode in which the child's mind is unfolded which would qualify them for presenting it, either as to matter or as to method, psychologically. There should be, therefore, some censorship which would guard the child from the evil effects of text-books defective in arrangement and matter and perhaps inaccurate as to statement of facts. This censorship the Education Department of Ontario assumes.

On the principle that no man can teach a school as well as the trained teacher, the department has assumed that no person can prepare a text-book except the person who has taught the subject of which it treats. Accordingly, when it is felt by experienced teachers that the textbook in any subject has outlived its usefulness, is deficient or redundant with regard to any part of the field which it is supposed to cover, or is wanting in logical arrangement, or is obsolete as to the theories which it propounds, it becomes the duty of the department to prepare a new text-book in such subject. In the discharge of this duty the department seeks out one or more teachers whose standing and experience are universally admitted, and intrusts to them the preparation of the book required. For instance, when it was found that the text-books authorized in 1867 in the subject of reading did not meet with the approval of the profession generally, a committee was appointed by the Minister of Education, consisting of three men of well-known ability and taste and with large experience as teachers, for the preparation of a new series of readers. One member of the committee was the holder of a degree from the provincial university, another an inspector of high standing, and the third a teacher of wide experience. The department placed at their disposal its reference library of 10,000 volumes, and supplied them with all the text-books in reading that could be obtained from the leading publishers of the United States and Great Britain. They were instructed to invite suggestions from the profession, and to read the works of the best authors on the subject of reading. For nearly two years they devoted themselves almost continuously to the duty assigned to them. Whatever illustrations were thought necessary were engraved from copies taken from other text-books or from original drawings prepared by the best artists available; and as the result of their labours, a series of readers has been placed in the schools which the profession has unanimously received with favour. The cost to the department was comparatively trifling, while the advantages to pupils and teachers were incalculable.

In the preparation of other text-books, such as arithmetic, grammar, or geography, a different course was pursued. In these cases a single teacher was advised that a text-book in the subject in which he was *facile princeps* was required, and, after consultation with the Minister of Education and well-known experts, he entered upon the task assigned to him. The manuscript was put in type by some printer or publisher selected for the purpose, and proofs were sent to a number of persons known to be capable teachers and critics, who were instructed to communicate with the author or the Minister of Education. Every part of the work was therefore subjected to the closest scrutiny; inaccuracies were sure to be detected and all reasonable doubts removed as to the usefulness of the work when completed. The cost of revising or even resetting the book three or four times, as has often happened, was considered a small matter where the interests of half a million children were involved. By the adoption of this course, the department has obtained in every subject text-books which are reasonably satisfactory, and which conform to sound principles of pedagogy as understood by the best members of the profession.

When a text-book is prepared by a single teacher or by one or more teachers without disturbing their professional engagements, instead of paying them a fixed sum of money for their work, they are allowed a royalty of ten per cent on the retail price of each book, such royalty to be paid by the publisher authorized by the department to place the book upon the market.

As a matter of practice the text-books in every subject except reading are revised decennially, and a notice of one or two years given to teachers and the publishing trade that a new text-book is forthcoming. The pupils are in this way protected against the purchase of books under the impression that their use will be continued, and the trade warned against the issue of a large edition which will be unsalable when a new book is authorized.

3. That Canadian authorship should be encouraged.

While the department holds itself free to authorize the best book in any subject, no matter where published, it is considered desirable to encourage the profession by the prospective rewards of authorship. The prizes in the profession are at best both limited in number and moderate as to value, and any incentive which authorship might afford is due to the men who may have given to the profession all their energy and talent. Where it is found, however, that a book of special value has been published, either in Great Britain or the United States, there is no hesitation in authorizing such book for the schools of Ontario. This applies particularly to text-books required in high schools, and to which the "one text-book" policy of the department is not so rigidly applied.

4. That the quality and price of text-books should be regulated.

When a text-book has been approved by the department it becomes the duty of the Minister of Education to find a publisher who will place the book upon the market. As the book is sure to have a wide sale, and there is no danger of any loss from depreciated stock, publishers are easily found to undertake this task, particularly as there is no competition and can be no competition with regard to the sale. Having found a publisher, the next duty is to settle the quality of the book as to paper, binding, etc., the character of the type to be used, and the price to the purchaser. Through an officer of the Government known as the Queen's Printer, who is charged with the publication of all parliamentary documents, and who is by virtue of his office an expert printer, the desired quality of paper, binding, typography, and price are easily adjusted; and as soon as an agreement is arrived at the publisher is required to enter into a contract with the department containing the following provisions:

1. That the publisher will, during the time such book is authorized, publish each and every edition of the book on the quality of paper and according to the style of binding approved of, and will not vary either during the period of authorization, under the penalty of having the right of publication withdrawn, or any book not published according to the standard confiscated by the department.

2. In order to enforce this agreement, the Minister of Education reserves to himself the right, through an officer appointed for the purpose, to examine all text-books during the process of manufacture as to the quality of paper used, the quality of the ink employed in printing, the material used in binding, and to see that in every detail the agreement is faithfully carried out. Should this officer find in the warehouse of any publisher books of inferior workmanship, he has power to prevent such books being placed upon the market; the loss in that case being the publisher's loss.

3. In order that the purchaser of the book may have no doubt as to the price he should pay for it, it is required by the department that the price at which the book is to be sold shall be stamped on the outside cover of the book in conspicuous figures; and in order that the retail trade may have a reasonable profit upon the sale of these books, the publisher is required to allow such discounts upon the retail price as may have been fixed by the Minister of Education. These discounts are graduated, according to trade usage, on the quantity sold to any purchaser.

4. As it may happen that during the time a book remains on the authorized list of text-books the cost of paper and labour may materially decline, the Minister of Education has power under the agreement with the publishers to vary the price at which the book was originally placed upon the market. This he is not supposed to do capriciously, but only upon due inquiry and with reasonable regard to the rights and interests of the publisher.

5. As the publisher of a text-book when first placed upon the market is usually put to some extra cost, in the matter of type-setting, making plates, etc., such original publisher is allowed the exclusive right to sell the book for a period of two or three years, the time depending upon the cost of preparation. At the end of that period any other publisher, on the permission of the Minister of Education and on entering into an agreement with the department, is allowed to publish such text-book. This is to prevent the monopoly of publication by one publishing house. It also encourages publishers, if they so desire and can afford it, to sell books at a lower price than that fixed by the department.

6. All text-books are authorized for a period of five years at least, and any text-book may be withdrawn by the Minister of Education at any time after five years on giving one year's notice to the publisher. In this way loss to the publisher and the public is guarded against.

7. As a guarantee that the contract entered into by the publisher with the Education Department will be carried out in good faith, the publisher is required to give security in a penal sum of $5,000.

The objections urged to the text-book policy of the Education Department are:

(*a*) That it discourages the production of original work.

In answer to this it may be said that any author is at liberty to publish any text-book and to promote its sale at pleasure among the teachers of the country. If it is found that a book published in this way is specially meritorious and commends itself to the profession, the Education Department is free to enter into any arrangement with the author of such a book for its use in the province. Originality is sure to meet with appreciation; but whatever loss occurs in this respect is more than compensated for by preventing useless and defective books from being forced upon Boards of Trustees and teachers by speculative publishers.

(*b*) It is said that this policy encourages monopoly and prevents the publication of low-priced books. The answer to this is that there can be no monopoly when the price is fixed by the department, and when all publishers after a limited time are permitted to publish any authorized text-book. As to quality, the policy of the department is equally effective; for a new publisher in order to promote the sale of a text-book may, if he desire, improve the quality of the paper, typography, or binding, and sell it at a price lower than that fixed by the department, as the department merely regulates the maximum price, not the minimum.

(*c*) It is said that this policy prevents such changes in text-books as improved methods of teaching might require. Not necessarily. As a matter of fact, it is found desirable to prevent too frequent changes of text-books and the consequent disorganization of schools. Besides, no publisher has a better opportunity of knowing the educational wants of the people than the Minister of Education through his inspectors and the profession with whom he comes continually in contact. In dealing with a question so closely connected with the education of the people, the responsibility of changing text-books should rest with some properly constituted authority, and not with those who might be influenced to suggest a change because of the material advantages thereby afforded.

It is true that this duty casts upon the department a great responsibility, but so does the duty of organizing a course of study, the duty of inspecting schools, and the duty of providing trained teachers. The limit of responsibility should be the public interests involved; and as the whole system of education might be vitiated by defective text-books, the Education Department would be unable to discharge its full responsibility to the public without dealing with the subject of text-books in the same careful and intelligent manner as it is expected to deal with all other subjects affecting the education of the people.

CHAPTER XI.

THE PROVINCIAL UNIVERSITY.

THE subject of higher education engaged the attention of the Legislature of Ontario from its earliest infancy. Even before his arrival in Ontario, Lieutenant-Governor Simcoe, the first Lieutenant-Governor of the Province, in a letter to Sir Joseph Banks, President of the Royal Society, said: " I should be glad to lay the foundation stone of some society that might hereafter conduce to the extension of science; a college of a higher class would be eminently useful, and would give a tone of principle and manners that would be of infinite support to the Government." And a month before the close of his official term he wrote to the Duke of Portland, Colonial Secretary, suggesting the appropriation of public lands for educational purposes, "the first and chief of which must be the erection and endowment of a university from which, more than any other source or circumstance whatever, a grateful attachment to his Majesty, morality, and religion, will be fostered and take root throughout the whole province."

Influenced no doubt by Lieutenant-Governor Simcoe's anxiety on behalf of education, the Legislature on the 3d of July, 1797, petitioned the Imperial Government to set apart a portion of the waste lands of the province " for the establishment of a respectable grammar school in each district thereof, and also of a college or university, where the youth of the country may be enabled to perfect themselves in the different branches of liberal knowledge." The petition of the Legislature was favourably entertained by the imperial authorities, and as a result 500,000 acres of the waste lands of the Crown were set apart for educational purposes, half of which was to be applied to the establishment and maintenance of a grammar school in each of the four districts into which the province was divided, and the other half for the maintenance of a university. The exact amount of land appropriated in consequence of this petition was 550,274 acres.

In 1825 it was suggested that as the lands appropriated were unsalable, a portion of them might be exchanged for other lands held by the Crown in older townships which had become comparatively valuable under the influence of settlement and cultivation; and in 1826 Dr. Strachan was sent to England to press on the attention of the Imperial Government the expediency of this course and the advisability of granting a royal charter for the establishment of the proposed university. In March, 1827, Dr. Strachan returned to Ontario, having in the meantime obtained a charter for the establishment of a university to be known as King's College. The lands intended for university purposes were vested in the corporation created by this charter; the charter was dated the 15th of March, 1827.

The university thus established was strictly sectarian in its control and management, and was in fact a university of the Church of England in Canada. The bishop of the diocese was made *ex officio* visitor of the college; the Archdeacon of York was made *ex officio* its president; each of the seven professors who were to be members of its council was required to be also a member of the "Established United Church of England and Ireland," and, before his admission into the college, "to sign and subscribe to the Thirty-nine Articles of Religion as declared and set forth in the Book of Common Prayer." Provision was made for the recognition of Divinity as one of the faculties, though no religious test or qualification was to be required of, or appointed for, any matriculant into any faculty except that of Divinity. In explanation of the fact that such a liberal public endowment should have been placed under the control of a single religious denomination, and of the still more singular fact that such a charter should have been put forward as "not only the most open charter for a university that had ever been granted, but the most liberal that could be framed on constitutional principles," it should be borne in mind that the Church of England was then virtually, if not legally, the established Church of Ontario, and that subscription to the Thirty-nine Articles was then required, not merely of all who had any share in the control of the Universities of Oxford and Cambridge, but of all who proposed to take a degree in any faculty.

The granting of a charter so exclusive in its privileges and so distinctly sectarian created great dissatisfaction in the province, and an appeal was made to the Imperial Parliament for such modifications as would enable all persons, irrespective of their denominational preferences, to avail themselves of the privileges which a university was intended to confer. The views of the Legislature on his point were so well expressed in the report of a committee appointed to consider the matter as to render them worthy of quotation. The committee said: " A university should not be a school of politics or of sectarian views.

It should have about it no appearance of partiality or exclusion. Its portals should be thrown open to all, and upon none who enter should any influence be exerted to attach them to a particular creed or church. It should be a source of intellectual and moral light and animation, from which the glorious irradiations of literature and science may descend upon all with equal lustre and power. Such an institution would be a blessing to a country, its pride and glory."

As a result of the controversies in the Legislature, the charter of King's College was suspended by Sir John Colborne, Lieutenant-Governor of the Province, and in 1829, by order of the Executive Government, a college known as Upper Canada College was founded and endowed with part of the land set apart for grammar schools and the university.

Act of 1837.—In the meantime the discussions with regard to the sectarian character of the charter of King's College occupied the attention of the Legislative Assembly. In 1837 a statute was passed removing the college from the direct control of the Anglican Church, and declaring that no religious test should be required of any person appointed on the college council or any professor appointed to the faculty "other than a declaration that they believe in the authenticity and divine inspiration of the Old and New Testaments, and the doctrine of the Trinity, and that no religious test or qualification be required for any person admitted or matriculated as scholars within the said college, or of persons admitted to any degree or faculty." *

---

* Although the university was generally declared to be non-sectarian, a chair in Divinity was still retained, and degrees in Divinity were to be conferred as in other courses of study.

THE PROVINCIAL UNIVERSITY. 177

Owing to political disturbances and other causes the erection of the necessary buildings for the university was delayed from time to time, but after an interval of nearly fifty years the good intentions of Lieutenant-Governor Simcoe were to be realized; and on the 23d of April, 1842, Sir Charles Bagot, Lieutenant-Governor of Canada, laid the foundation stone of the University of King's College in what is now known as Queen's Park in the city of Toronto. On the 8th of June, pending the completion of the building, the first session of the university was held in the old Parliament buildings, with an enrolment of thirty-one students.

Act of 1849.—In 1849 an act was passed which completely secularized King's College, and changed its name to the University of Toronto. By this act the Governor-General of the Province was made visitor, the chancellor was to be elected triennially by the Convocation, and the vice-chancellor biennially by the Senate. The three faculties of law, medicine, and arts were organized under deans of their own appointment, and authorized to enact by-laws for their own government, subject to the confirmation of the Senate. The general government and discipline of the university, in subordination to the Senate, was vested in a "caput" composed of five members, the president of the university, the three deans of faculties, and a representative elected by convocation. An endowment board was also provided for the management of the funds of the university. A Senate was created to which were intrusted all the academic interests of the university.

In order to make it perfectly clear that the university was entirely relieved of all denominational taint, it was provided that the chancellor should not be "a minister or ecclesiastical teacher under or according to any form of religious faith whatsoever." A similar restriction was placed upon the Government in its appointment of members of the Senate. The faculty of Divinity, and with it the professorship of the same subject, was abolished, and the right to confer degrees in Divinity was expressly abrogated.

Act of 1853.—In 1853 the University Act was further amended, and several important changes were made: 1. Following the example of the University of London, England, the examining and teaching functions of the university were separated, the former being vested in the University of Toronto, and the latter in a separate body created by the act, known as University College. 2. The teaching faculties of law and medicine were abolished, and the work of the university strictly limited to instruction in arts. 3. The chancellor of the university was to be appointed by the Executive Government, and the vice-chancellor elected biennially by the Senate. 4. The functions of the Senate were limited to the conducting of the examination for degrees and the transaction of such business as pertained to the academic requirements of the university. 5. All incorporated colleges in Ontario and Quebec were affiliated with the university for examination purposes, and power was given the Executive Government to declare what other arts colleges, and to the Senate what schools of law or medicine, should be admitted to a similar privilege. 6. The discipline of the professors, students, and officers of the university was vested in the Council of University College. 7. The perfect freedom of professors or students from all religious or denominational tests was reasserted. 8. The endowment and other property of the university was placed in the hands of an officer called the bursar, appointed by the Executive Government.

Act of 1873.—In 1873 Convocation was re-established, and the right of the alumni to elect the chancellor and certain members of the Senate recognised. In 1885, by resolution of the Legislative Assembly, women were admitted to the university on the same terms and with the same privileges as the other sex.*

The Federation Act of 1887.—In the desire to raise the standard. of university education it was felt that better results would be obtained by concentrating provincial effort in one central university rather than diffusing it among outlying universities whose endowments were unequal to the greatly expanded course of study furnished by the universities of other countries.

Accordingly, by the Act of 1887, provision was made whereby any chartered university might hold in abeyance its power for granting degrees. Its students in that case would attend the lectures in part of their course, at least, at the provincial university, and on passing the required examinations would receive their degrees as of the provincial university. The federation which was thus proposed was ineffectual except in so far as relates to Victoria University, which removed its headquarters from Cobourg—a town about sixty miles east from Toronto—and erected new buildings in the city of Toronto, in 1892. The other universities still continue to do full university work under their own charters.

---

* The other universities of Ontario are: Victoria University (Methodist); Trinity University, Toronto (Anglican); McMaster, Toronto (Baptist); Queen's University, Kingston (Presbyterian); Regiopolis, Kingston (Roman Catholic), suspended; Ottawa University (Roman Catholic); Western University, London.

A material change also was made in the constitution of the university in other respects. As already pointed out, the university proper was an examining body similar to the University of London, England—all instruction being given in what was known as University College. By the Act of 1887 this distinction between the university and University College was abolished, and although the functions of University College were retained as a matter of law, yet the distinction between the two bodies is now more technical than real. The faculties of medicine and law, which were abolished by the Act of 1853, were also revived.

Government of the University.—The government of the University of Toronto is somewhat complex. The supreme control, both as to its finances and academic business is vested in the Executive Government of the Province. Although the Senate, the trustees, Convocation, and the university and college councils have certain powers, yet in all matters of importance which these various bodies are intrusted to deal with the approval of the Government must be obtained.

The Lieutenant-Governor of the Province is the visitor of the university, and has the right by commission to inquire into any matter which, in his opinion, affects its interests. All the property of the university is vested in the Government, and is managed by an officer appointed by the Government called a bursar. The bursar is assisted in his duties by a Board of Trustees consisting of nine members—viz., the chancellor, the vice-chancellor, and the president of University College, five members elected by the Senate of the university and one by the council of University College. The trustees exercise a general control over the expenditure on maintenance and equipment, the erection of such additional buildings as may be approved of by the Government, and the endowment funds of the university. Their annual estimate of the money required for carrying on the work of the university is subject to the approval of the Government.

Faculty, how appointed.—The faculty consists of professors, associate professors, lecturers, instructors, demonstrators, etc. The academic head of the university is called the president. All appointments to the teaching staff (the president included) are made by the Government after such inquiry as to fitness as may be deemed expedient. These appointments are during pleasure. The Government has the right to dismiss any member of the teaching staff for cause at any time, and the Senate has the right by committee to inquire into the efficiency of any member of the teaching staff, and to report the results of such inquiry to the Government.*

The Senate.—The Senate consists of three classes of members: 1, *ex-officio* members; 2, appointed members; 3, elected members. The *ex-officio* members are the Minister of Education, the president of the university, the president or head of each federated university or college, the chancellor and vice-chancellor, and all past chancel-

---

* Salaries in the provincial university are graduated as follows: For a lecturer, an initial salary of $1,000, with an increase of $100 a year until the maximum of $1,800 is reached; for an associate professor, an initial salary of $1,800, with an increase of $100 a year until the maximum of $2,500 is reached; for a professor, an initial salary of $2,500, with an increase of $100 until a maximum of $3,200 is reached; the salary of the president is $5,000 a year. Instructors and demonstrators are paid salaries varying according to the importance of the duties to which they are assigned.

lors and vice-chancellors. The appointed members consist of three representatives of the council of the University of Toronto—one from the council of University College, one from the Law Society of Upper Canada, one from each federated or affiliated institution, and nine members appointed by the Executive Government. The elected members number twenty-three, and represent the graduates of the federated universities in arts (seventeen members), in medicine (four members), in law (two members). Elections take place to the Senate every three years. The mode of election is as follows: Any ten members of Convocation—i. e., any ten graduates—may deposit with the registrar a nomination paper containing the names of such persons as they desire to see elected to the Senate. These names are transmitted by the registrar to every graduate whose address is known, and at a time specified in the act the graduate returns his voting paper to the registrar, and in presence of scrutineers appointed for that purpose the votes are counted, and the persons having the majority are declared elected as members of the Senate.

The chancellor of the university is elected in the same way by the whole body of graduates. The vice-chancellor is appointed triennially at the first meeting of the new Senate. The Senate has by statute the right to determine the standards for matriculation into the university, the standards for the examination to be taken for each year or for any degree which the university is authorized to confer, the right to appoint the examiners for preparing and reading the papers of students in every department of university work, and generally to decide upon all academic matters subject to the approval of the Executive Government of the province.

Matriculation.—By means of a joint Board of Examiners, four of whom are appointed by the Senate and four by the Education Department, an examination is annually conducted for matriculation. Candidates who pass this examination are recognised as having obtained the standing required of second-class teachers, in addition to the privilege of admission into the university. The subjects of examination are: Latin, English, history, mathematics, French or German, and either (1) Greek or (2) the second modern language with physics and chemistry. This examination is conducted simultaneously with the examinations of the Education Department for teachers' certificates. In the case of candidates who fail in not more than three subjects, a supplemental examination may be taken in the month of September, in the subjects in which they fail.

Course of Study.—The course of study in the faculty of arts consists of Latin, Greek, French, German, Italian, Spanish, and Hebrew, with so much ancient history and geography as incidentally pertain to the study of the languages. In science: Physics, mineralogy, geology, biology, chemistry, and psycho-physics. In philosophy: The history of philosophy, logic, ethics, metaphysics, and psychology. In English: Modern history, comparative philology, and English literature and education. In political science: Political economy, constitutional history, constitutional and international law, Roman law, and general jurisprudence. The teaching staff in the faculty of arts consists of thirteen professors, four associate professors, and twenty-six lecturers and demonstrators.

Faculty of Medicine.—In the faculty of medicine the course of study is similar to that pursued in all well-organized medical schools. The students in this faculty have free access to the well-equipped laboratories of the university for conducting experiments in morphology, physiological chemistry, botany, psychology, and chemistry. The teaching staff in the faculty of medicine consists of fifteen professors, three associate professors, and twenty-one lecturers and demonstrators.

Owing to the want of funds, no faculty in law has yet been organized.

Affiliated Universities and Colleges.—Since its first incorporation, the University of Toronto invited affiliation with other educational institutions, and from year to year steadily enlarged its relations in this respect until they now include Victoria University (Methodist), Knox College (Presbyterian), Wycliffe College (Anglican), St. Michael's College (Roman Catholic), Albert College (Methodist), Huron College (Anglican), Trinity Medical College, the Woman's Medical College, the School of Pharmacy, the School of Dentistry, the Provincial School of Practical Science, the Provincial College of Agriculture, and the Toronto College of Music. These institutions are entitled to representation on the Senate, and to share in the administration of the university. Examinations for degrees in all federated or affiliated colleges or universities are conducted by the University of Toronto, excepting for degrees in theology.

The Library.—The university library occupies a separate fireproof building with a storage capacity of 120,000 volumes, and a reading room capable of seating upward of 200 readers. The library contains about 55,000 volumes and about 5,000 unbound pamphlets. The library is a circulating one for members of the faculties, and a library of reference for students. For the purpose of instruction on the seminary method, special rooms are set apart for the professors and students in each department of study, the works of reference required for the course being placed in such rooms. There are two large museums, one illustrative of the course in biology, and the other of the course in ethnology.

Gymnasium.—A gymnasium costing about $30,000 has been fitted up for the benefit of students with all suitable appliances for athletic purposes. In connection with the gymnasium, rooms are set apart for the meetings of students' clubs and societies, including a large hall for public meetings, a reading room, and committee rooms.

Degrees.—Degrees in arts are conferred on those persons who have completed the prescribed course of study and who have passed the required examinations. The course extends over four years, and is divided into general and special courses. A corresponding distinction is made in the degrees conferred. Attendance at lectures is compulsory unless a dispensation is granted by the Senate owing to special circumstances. The degree of Master of Arts is conferred upon Bachelors of Arts of at least two years' standing on the presentation of an approved thesis in one of the departments in arts. Provision is made for admission *ad eundem gradum* in the case of both degrees. In 1895 the Senate passed a statute to confer the degree of Bachelor of Pedagogy and Doctor of Pedagogy on teachers who passed the prescribed examination.

Discipline.—The discipline of the university is vested in the president and faculty of University College. Matriculated students are required to attend the courses of study and examinations in all subjects prescribed for students of their respective standing. No student is permitted to remain in the college who persistently neglects academic work, or whose presence is deemed prejudicial to the interests of the university. "Hazing" is strictly forbidden. No suspended student may be admitted to the university buildings or grounds. No person is allowed to lecture before any of the university societies without the approval of the university council. Men and women students, unless members of the same family, are not permitted to reside in the same lodging houses. Women students are under the supervision of a lady superintendent, and are subject to her directions as to their conduct in the university halls and lecture rooms, or while attending university societies.

College Residence.—The residential quarters of the university are very limited in extent, capable of accommodating only between forty and fifty students. The residence is in charge of a dean, who has the oversight of students in residence. The regulations for the government and discipline of the college are prescribed by the college council.

Devotional exercises are conducted in the college by the dean. Devotional exercises are also conducted in the university daily at ten o'clock; attendance is not compulsory in either case, but those who have no conscientious scruples are expected to be present.

The fees chargeable for attendance upon lectures average about $40 per student.

The School of Science.—The School of Science was erected on the grounds of the university, in order that the students of the school might conveniently receive instruction from the professors of the university, and also that the students of the university might avail themselves of the laboratories of the School of Science. The school is affiliated with the university, and represented by its principal on the Senate. The buildings and equipment cost about $250,000. The faculty consists of three professors, five lecturers, six fellows, and an assistant in each of the departments of chemistry and metallurgy. The teaching staff is appointed by the Government. The school is under the direction of the Minister of Education, and in that respect is part of the school system of the province. It is modelled after the Boston School of Technology. Its course includes surveying, architecture, applied mechanics, applied chemistry, civil engineering, mechanical engineering, electrical engineering, mineralogy, metallurgy, and assaying.

A special examination is conducted by the faculty of the school in arithmetic, algebra, Euclid, and English for the admission of students, but any person who has passed the matriculation examination of the University is eligible for admission. The course of study extends over three years. The fees are $45 per annum. The average attendance of students is from one hundred to one hundred and forty. Students who take a post-graduate course of one year and pass the required examinations are eligible for the degree of Bachelor of Applied Science in the University of Toronto. Graduates in the department of civil engineering are eligible for the degree of Civil Engineer, after three years of practical work.

CHAPTER XII.

GROWTH OF THE ONTARIO SCHOOL SYSTEM.

IT was not until the school system of Ontario was organized under the Act of 1843 that any regular effort was made to compile the returns received from superintendents and other school officers. The earliest reliable reports begin with the year 1844. These reports show that up to that time there had been established 2,610 public schools, with a registered attendance of 96,756 pupils, in charge of 2,736 teachers. In the fifty years that have elapsed since 1844 the schools have increased to 5,649, the registered pupils to 483,203, and the teachers to 8,824, of whom 2,795 were males and 6,029 females. The returns do not show the establishment of any Roman Catholic separate schools as early as 1844, although there is no doubt that many schools were, under the Act of 1843, conducted as separate schools. The number of high schools, then called grammar schools, was 25, with an attendance of about 3,000 pupils.

One of the most significant indications of the development of the school system of the province is the steady increase in the average attendance of pupils. This may be partly owing to improved facilities for transportation and partly to the improvement in the circumstances of the people, by which parents and guardians are better able to dispense with the labour of the pupils, particularly in rural districts. In 1867, out of 401,643 children registered, the average attendance was forty-one per cent; in 1894 the average attendance had risen to fifty-six per cent. By way of explanation, it should be said, however, that the average attendance in Ontario is determined, not by the number of days each school is kept open, but by the number of teaching days in the academic year. For instance, a school running six months, with an average attendance of 40 pupils per day, would in the official return show an average attendance of only fifty per cent for the year. The average attendance in rural districts in 1894 was fifty-one per cent, in cities sixty-nine per cent, and in towns sixty-four per cent; in some individual cases the average reached seventy-nine per cent.

Classification of Pupils.—By the system of classification fixed by the Education Department a pupil's whole course of study is determined by the form to which he has been promoted. It is only in the fifth or highest form that options are allowed. It follows, therefore, that any increase in the number of pupils studying any subject depends to a great extent upon the increased attendance of registered pupils. The changes in the courses of study, however, since 1867, have largely affected the number of pupils in some subjects. Drawing, which was optional in 1867, is now compulsory, and the number of pupils in this subject has increased since that time from 5,450 to 435,541. In the same way English and Canadian history occupied relatively an inferior place in the course of study; recent changes in the regulations of the department have increased the number of pupils in this subject from 61,787 in 1867 to 264,896. Similarly in the subject of music the increase has been from 47,618 to 206,346. The study of physiology and temperance was also optional till 1885, and is now studied from text-books and charts by 191,406 pupils. The following statement shows the enrolment of pupils in the subjects mentioned:

Bookkeeping	22,422	Botany	6,122
Algebra	13,353	Elementary physics	3,549
Geometry	12,693	Agriculture	7,680

Taking the whole enrolment of the public schools of the province, the percentages in the various subjects of the course of study are as follows:

	Per cent.		Per cent.
Reading	100	Grammar and composition	63
Writing	96	English history	23
Arithmetic	98	Canadian history	32
Drawing	90	Physiology and temperance	40
Geography	70	Drill and calisthenics	49
Music	41		

Perhaps the most satisfactory test of the efficiency of the public-school system is the annual departmental examination required for entrance to high schools. As stated elsewhere, this examination is usually taken at the end of the fourth form. In 1877, 3,836 pupils, as compared with 10,049 pupils in 1895, were successful at this examination.

Teaching Staff.—Although the number of schools in the province has more than doubled within the last fifty years, there has been scarcely any increase in the number of male teachers employed. As stated above, the number of male teachers in 1844 was 2,736; fifty years later—in 1894—the number was 2,795, whereas in the same period of time female teachers, unknown to the profession in 1844, increased to 6,029. The increase in the number of female teachers employed is greater in urban than in rural districts, although even in the latter case they preponderate. The effect of this transfer of the educational work of the

GROWTH OF THE ONTARIO SCHOOL SYSTEM. 191

country from the male sex to the female sex can not be discussed here; it may be said, however, that so far there is no perceptible deterioration in the quality of the work done in the schoolroom, while in the matter of discipline and in all the other circumstances which go to make school life pleasant to the pupil, there has been a very marked improvement. The average age of the teachers employed is nearly twenty-six years (25·95), and their average experience four years and three fifths. The number holding first-class certificates—the highest certificate granted by the department—is 262; the number holding second-class certificates 3,184; the remainder hold certificates of lower grades.

As to professional training there is a very gratifying and steady increase. In 1867 the number of teachers who had attended a normal school was 666; in 1894 this number had arisen to 3,207. Nearly forty per cent of all the teachers of the province have attended a normal school; of the remainder the greater number have received professional training at a county model school.

The increase in teachers' salaries has not kept pace with their professional attainments and is far from satisfactory. The average salary of a male teacher in the whole province in 1867 was $346, and in 1894 $421. The average salary of a female teacher was $226, and in 1894 $300. The average salary of male teachers in rural districts in 1894 was $376, and of female teachers $269; the average salary of male teachers in cities $876, and of female teachers $415. The average salary of male teachers in towns was $632, and of female teachers $303. The highest salary paid a teacher in a public school was $1,500.

Maintenance of Public Schools.—The total expenditure upon public schools in 1867 was $1,473,000, or an average of $3.67 per pupil. In 1894 the expenditure had increased to $4,248,000, or an average of $8.79 per pupil. Of this expenditure the sum of $300,000 was contributed by the Legislature of Ontario and the sum of $3,460,000 was raised by assessment on the taxable property of the ratepayers. The amount expended on teachers' salaries was $2,822,000; on maps and apparatus, $50,465; on sites and buildings, $445,000; and on general expenses, $870,000. The estimated value of public-school property in 1894 was $10,600,000.

Roman Catholic Separate Schools.—The reports of the Education Department show that in 1854 there were 44 Roman Catholic separate schools in the province; in 1867 the separate schools numbered 161, attended by 18,924 pupils; the number at the close of 1894 was 328, attended by 39,762 pupils. In 1867 the number of teachers employed was 210; in 1894 the number increased to 714, of whom 323 were lay teachers and 391 religious teachers—that is, teachers belonging to some religious order of the Roman Catholic Church. The number of pupils in the various subjects in the separate-school course of study bears the same proportion to the whole number in attendance as in the case of public schools, the classification and optional subjects being the same.

High Schools.—The growth of the high-school system of the province since 1867 has been very satisfactory, as the following statement shows:

	1867.	1894.
Number of schools	103	129
Number of teachers	159	554
Number of pupils	5,696	23,523
Cost per pupil	$21 80	$29 27
Total expenditures	$124,181	$682,532
Paid for salaries	$94,820	$507,441
Government grant	$54,562	$100,000

GROWTH OF THE ONTARIO SCHOOL SYSTEM. 193

Classification.—The classification of high-school pupils is largely determined by the course of study required for matriculation into the university. The following table, therefore, to a certain extent, indicates the trend of secondary education in the province:

CLASSIFICATION OF HIGH-SCHOOL PUPILS, 1867-'94.

	1867.	1894.
Composition and rhetoric	4,091	23,360
Poetical literature	....	23,416
History	4,634	23,260
Geography	5,264	23,418
Arithmetic	5,526	22,404
Algebra	2,841	23,253
Euclid	1,847	20,569
Trigonometry	141	1,353
Physics	1,876	7,335
Chemistry	840	4,880
Botany	....	6,088
Latin	5,171	9,366
Greek	802	1,080
French	2,164	10,530
German	....	2,785
Drawing	676	14,827
Commercial subjects	1,283	15,101

From the above table it will be observed that English and English literature are receiving increased attention, partly by the addition of poetical literature to the course of study and partly by the expansion of the subjects of composition and rhetoric. Nor has the mathematical group of studies been neglected, as may be seen from the large increase in the number of pupils in algebra, Euclid, and trigonometry. A similar remark will apply to the science group, and particularly to the subjects of chemistry and botany. The desire to meet a popular demand for what is called a practical education (what that means it is hard to say) has led to the establishment of a commercial course in high schools. This accounts for the large increase in the number of pupils in commercial subjects. The language group is somewhat influenced by the elective principle for matriculation, and therefore indicates to a certain extent the preferences of pupils and teachers. In 1867 ninety per cent of the whole attendance at the high schools of the province studied Latin; in 1894 the number of Latin pupils was only forty per cent of the number in attendance. In 1867 fifteen per cent of the pupils studied Greek, and in 1894 only five per cent. In 1867 thirty-eight per cent of the pupils studied French and none studied German; in 1894 these numbers had increased to forty-five per cent and twelve per cent respectively.

Although the high-school course is necessarily taken by persons looking forward to a professional career, it is worthy of notice that many take the course for the sake of the intellectual culture which it provides. From the reports of high-school principals in the offices of the department, it appears that since 1872 18,709 pupils have taken a high-school course with a view to prepare themselves for mercantile life, and 14,486 left the high school for agricultural pursuits.

As a test of the efficiency of the high schools it may be stated that in 1867, 56 pupils passed the matriculation examination required by the university. In 1894, 482 pupils passed this test, while 1,990 obtained third-class literary standing at the departmental examinations, 1,147 second-class literary standing, and 302 first-class literary standing.

The average salary of principals of high schools in 1895 was $1,065, and of principals of collegiate institutes $1,573. The highest salary paid in the whole province was $2,500.

Training of Teachers.—County model schools for the training of teachers of third-class literary standing were first established in 1877, and were attended that year by 1,146 teachers in training. The attendance increased to 1,834 in 1895, and the number of model schools from fifty to sixty. The average salary paid the principal of a model school is $844. The number of normal-school students has increased from 257 in 1877 to 442 in 1895, and the expenditure on normal schools, etc., from $25,780 to $52,668. The maximum salary of normal-school principals is $2,500, and of assistants is $2,000. The salaries paid teachers in the model or practice schools attached to the provincial normal schools are graduated according to a scale determined by the Education Department. The first two years of service are considered probationary. At the end of this time an annual increase of $50 is allowed until the maximum fixed by the department is reached. For head masters the minimum is $1,300, and the maximum $1,500; for head mistresses and male assistants the minimum is $1,000, and the maximum $1,200; for female assistants the minimum is $650, and the maximum $850; for directors of kindergartens, music masters, and drawing masters the minimum is $800, and the maximum $1,000. The principal of the Ontario Normal College (School of Pedagogy) is paid a salary of $3,000, and the vice principal $2,300 per annum.

The number of teachers' institutes has increased from forty-two in 1877 to seventy-three in 1894, and the number of teachers in attendance from 1,181 in the same year to 7,630, representing over ninety per cent of all the teachers of the province. The expenditure upon teachers' institutes in 1894 was $6,527, of which sum $2,000 was spent on reference libraries. The directors of teachers' institutes and the inspectors of model schools are each paid $1,850 annually and travelling expenses.

Public Libraries.—The following table shows the number of public libraries in 1883 and 1895:

	1883.	1895.
Number of public libraries...............	93	300
Number of reading rooms................	59	192
Number of newspapers and periodicals....	1,540	5,136
Number of volumes in libraries..........	154,093	604,719
Number of volumes issued...............	251,920	1,687,806
Total receipts........................	$59,716	$165,282
Total assets.........................	$255,190	$752,426

Arbor Day.—The number of trees planted since the establishment of Arbor Day was as follows:

In 1885................	38,940	In 1890................	22,250
" 1886................	34,087	" 1891................	15,697
" 1887................	25,057	" 1892................	14,489
" 1888................	25,714	" 1893................	14,103
" 1889................	21,281	" 1894................	14,244

Illiteracy.—From the decennial census of 1891 it appears that the percentage of the population of the Province of Ontario over twenty years of age, able to write, was 90·4; able to write between ten and twenty years, 94·22, or a higher percentage than obtained in any of the other provinces. The criminal statistics, however, do not show any material reduction in crime, except in the arrests for drunkenness.

Higher Education.—The progress of higher education, so far as high schools are concerned, has already been considered. The effect of their growth on the provincial university and its affiliated institutions has been to broaden the course of instruction, to re-enforce the staff by additional professors and lecturers in every department of study, and to increase the attendance of students in a corresponding degree.

In the academic year 1884–'85 the number of students taking an art course in the University of Toronto was 348; in 1895–'96 the number had increased to 875. In its affiliated institutions an equally gratifying increase has taken place in the number of students.

Briefly summed up, it may be said that the school system of the Province of Ontario takes in hand the child of four years of age at the kindergarten, and watches over his education for a period varying from eighteen to twenty years, or practically to the close of his professional training. If at the end of the public-school course he considers his education complete and goes no further, he finds himself reasonably well equipped for the duties of citizenship. If he pursues his studies until the end of the high-school course, he has acquired a wide knowledge of English literature, science, and mathematics, and one or more foreign languages. If he has chosen for himself a professional career, the provincial university, either through its own faculty or the faculties of affiliated institutions, offers him substantial facilities for achieving success and perhaps distinction in the profession of his choice.

APPENDIX.

Report on the Sanitary Condition of Rural Schools.

IN the autumn of 1895, searching inquiry was made by the department, through the inspectors, with regard to the health of teachers and pupils, and the sanitary condition of rural schools. As the inspectors were not able in the term to complete their inspection of all the rural schools, the report is incomplete. Nevertheless, it may be accepted as reasonably conclusive with regard to all matters to which it refers. The following schedule was filled up by the inspector on his visit to each school, from which the summary for his district was afterward made :

SPECIAL REPORT ON THE SANITARY CONDITION OF RURAL SCHOOLS.

Report on Teacher.

Name of teacher.................. ....: age........ ; years' experience........ ; would you consider teachers' health as excellent, good, or inferior................. ; number of days lost by illness in 1895......... ; was illness caused by any schoolroom defect............ ; does teacher take luncheon in schoolroom .... ; has teacher any fixed rules for exercise.......... ; does teacher go out of doors at recess.......... ; at noon.........

Report on Pupils.

Number of boys present........ ; girls........ ; how many boys would you rate as in feeble health........... ; girls.......... ; how many wear glasses.......... ; how many of defective hearing........ ; how many are indifferent to games and play........ ; are pupils more easily managed in the forenoon or afternoon...... .... ; how many take luncheon in the schoolroom

APPENDIX. 199

.........; what sports do boys favour.....................;
what sports do girls favour...................; number of properly organized sporting clubs among boys............; number of matches played by school in 1895.........; any epidemic among pupils in 1895..........; of what nature......................;
number who complain of headaches.........

Report on Schoolhouse.

Size of schoolhouse..............; material..............; are cubic contents sufficient for average attendance..............; do. for enrolment..............; has school building porch or anteroom...............; when was schoolroom last whitewashed ....; when was floor last scrubbed...............; how often swept...............; by whom swept...............; what provision made by trustees for scrubbing and sweeping...... ....; cost of...............; are seats graduated in height ....; are seats of good form and comfortable............; are rooms properly lighted..............; are windows provided with blinds in good order..............; are windows on weights ....; any structural provision for ventilation...........; are stoves and pipes in good repair and cleanly................

Report on School Grounds.

Is position of school site with respect to elevation of the ground, safety from malaria from swamps, and suitability for its purpose (having regard to the health and comfort of the pupils), excellent, good, bad; is condition of fence excellent, good, or bad; condition of gates excellent, good, or bad; are proper walks made from gates to schoolhouse door....................; are grounds level and dry and suitable for playgrounds................; number of shade trees that appear healthy..........; number flower beds..........; is well on the premises..........; is it in a sanitary location and condition.............; are there separate closets for the sexes ....; how many screened..........; how many have plank or gravel approaches...........; are they regularly disinfected ....; how often does teacher inspect them............; in good condition at date of visit..........; any woodshed.........; area of grounds..............

In connection with the above schedule, instructions,

signed by the Minister of Education, were sent to inspecttors as follows:

"As several of the answers to the inquiries in the schedule sent herewith can not be conveniently tabulated, I shall feel greatly obliged if you will summarize your observations upon the answers received in a few paragraphs supplementary to the statistical report. For instance, in your report on teachers I would like to have the general result of the information obtained with respect to the health of teachers, the effect of the schoolroom upon their powers of endurance, the ailments incident to the profession, and the care taken by teachers to maintain unimpaired their physical powers. I would like to know to what extent teachers suffer from the effects of bad ventilation or the unsanitary condition of the schoolroom, and if in your opinion there is any disease peculiar to the teaching profession, such as myopia, or bronchitis, or phthisis, or any neurotic trouble which could be mitigated by greater care on their own part or on the part of the school authorities. It is important to know whether the conditions under which the teacher pursues his profession are as favourable to the full enjoyment of health as they should be, both for his own sake and for the proper discharge of the public service which he is called upon to perform.

"In answer to the questions with regard to pupils, I should also desire your opinion on a number of points. For instance, are spectacles more used by pupils now than they were ten years ago? Do children show signs of spinal curvature or rounded shoulders, or any other physical defect which you think greater vigilance could prevent? It is also important to study carefully the evil effects which overcrowding and bad ventilation have upon the pupils' powers of study, upon their temper, and their desire to enjoy themselves. My reference to games and sports is to draw out the teachers with regard to the development of those manly sports without which a boy's education even at an ordinary public school is incomplete. No teacher should neglect the organization of clubs for cricket, baseball, football, etc. The training which a boy gets on the playground is just as useful as any part of his school course, not simply because it is healthful, but because it develops his self-control, his powers of self-defence, and his mettle in competing for the mastery in an honourable way over his fellows.

" In reporting upon schoolhouses I would like to know particularly as to the arrangements made for sweeping, scrubbing, and whitewashing. I fear these elementary principles of cleanliness are very much neglected in many school sections. It is hard to realize what injury may accrue to pupils and teachers from the polluted dust with which the atmosphere of many schoolrooms is loaded. The seeds of such diseases as diphtheria, scarlet fever, typhoid fever, or consumption may through this medium be transferred to many a promising pupil and teacher, with the most disastrous results.

"The examination of the school grounds is most important. Are they tidy and well kept? Are they mud puddles in spring and fall, or are they well drained, and with proper walks? Are they neatly fenced and planted with trees? Are they large enough for playground purposes, or are the pupils obliged to play upon the highways, etc.? But what is most important is the sanitary condition of the closets. I fear there is an amount of neglect in this respect in many parts of the province that must react upon the morals as well as upon the health of many pupils.

Let there be no sparing this evil if it exists. Deal with it fully and fearlessly."

The result of this inquiry is contained in the following statement:

SUMMARY REPORT ON THE SANITARY CONDITION OF THE RURAL SCHOOLS OF ONTARIO, 1895.

Total number of schools reported	3,794
" " " rural schools in Ontario	4,749

The Teachers.

Male teachers in schools inspected	1,703
Female teachers in schools inspected	2,297
Average age (male and female)	25·95
Average years' experience	4·6
Days lost by sickness	4,314
Cases of sickness chargeable to schoolroom	37
Number of teachers who take regular exercise	2,297
Health of teachers, excellent	2,271
" " " good	1,645
" " " inferior	141

The Schoolhouse.

School rooms below regulations in cubic contents	490
Number without porch	1,307
" " " or anteroom	769
Schools not whitewashed, 1895	1,820
Not scrubbed, 1895	265
Not swept daily	405
Number in which seats are defective	713
" without suitable or sufficient blinds	916
" " windows on weights	2,613
" " structural ventilation	2,341
Stoves and fixtures in bad repair	352
Schoolhouses, grade I	1,366
" " II	1,875
" " III	613

APPENDIX.

The Pupils.

Boys present	58,474
Girls "	60,707
Number who wear glasses	680
" defective hearing	1,005
" apparently weakly	1,966
" who complain of headaches	4,981
" indifferent to play	1,866
" who luncheon in school	92,001
Organized sporting clubs	316
Cases of epidemic diseases	919

The School Grounds.

Schools on a sanitary site, excellent	80
" " " " good	1,317
" " " " inferior	257
Fences and gates, excellent	1,243
" " " good	1,698
" " " inferior	824
Number with walks where required	1,552
" of growing shade trees	50,449
Wells in good condition	1,937
Number with separate closets	3,535
" not screened	2,343
" in good condition at date of visit	2,908
Woodsheds	2,459
Average area of grounds	.02 acre
School grounds, grade I	1,228
" " " II	1,803
" " " III	775

THE END.

D. APPLETON & CO.'S PUBLICATIONS.

NEW VOLUMES IN THE INTERNATIONAL EDUCATION SERIES.

THE SONGS AND MUSIC OF FROEBEL'S MOTHER PLAY. Prepared and arranged by SUSAN E. BLOW. Fully illustrated. Vol. 32, International Education Series. 12mo. Cloth, $1.50.

This is the second and concluding volume of Miss Blow's version of Froebel's noted work which laid the foundation for that important branch of early education, the kindergarten. The first volume, "The Mottoes and Commentaries," may be designated as the Teacher's or Mother's book, and "The Songs and Music," the present volume, as the Children's book. In the latter many of the pictures have been enlarged in parts to bring out the details more distinctly. New translations are made of the songs, eliminating the crudities of poetic composition that have appeared in the literal imitations of Froebel, and new music is substituted where the original has been discarded.

THE MOTTOES AND COMMENTARIES OF FRIEDRICH FROEBEL'S MOTHER PLAY. " Mother Communings and Mottoes" rendered into English verse by HENRIETTA R. ELIOT, and "Prose Commentaries" translated by SUSAN E. BLOW. With 48 full-page Illustrations. 12mo. Cloth, $1.50.

The increased interest in kindergarten work and the demand for a clearer exposition of Froebel's philosophy than has heretofore appeared have made a new version of the "Mother Play" an imperative necessity. No one is better equipped for such a work than Miss Blow, as her late book, "Symbolic Education," has attested. It is an attractive volume of a convenient size, and a book of specific value to mothers as well as to teachers of every grade. It will be followed shortly by another volume containing the songs and games.

FRIEDRICH FROEBEL'S PEDAGOGICS OF THE KINDERGARTEN; or, His Ideas concerning the Play and Playthings of the Child. Translated by JOSEPHINE JARVIS. 12mo. Cloth, $1.50.

This book holds the keynote of the "New Education," and will assist many in a correct comprehension of the true principles underlying the practical outcome of Froebel's thought. Although extant for nearly fifty years, his ideas are still in need of elucidation, and the average kindergartner and primary-school teacher grasps but a superficial meaning of the methods suggested.

THE PSYCHOLOGY OF NUMBER, and its Application to Methods of Teaching Arithmetic. By JAMES A. MCLELLAN, A. M., LL. D., Principal of the Ontario School of Pedagogy, Toronto, and JOHN DEWEY, Ph. D., Head Professor of Philosophy in the University of Chicago. 12mo. Cloth, $1.50.

It is believed that this work will supply a special want. There is no subject taught in the elementary schools that taxes the teacher's resources as to methods and devices to a greater extent than arithmetic, and none that is more dangerous to the pupil in the way of deadening his mind and arresting its development, if bad methods are used. The authors of this book have presented in an admirable manner the psychological view of number, and shown its applications to the correct methods of teaching the several arithmetical processes.

New York: D. APPLETON & CO., 72 Fifth Avenue.

D. APPLETON & CO.'S PUBLICATIONS.

RECENT VOLUMES OF THE INTERNATIONAL SCIENTIFIC SERIES.

MOVEMENT. By E. J. MAREY, Member of the Institute and of the Academy of Medicine; Professor at the College of France; author of "Animal Mechanism." Translated by Eric Pritchard, M. A. With 200 Illustrations. Vol. 73, International Scientific Series. 12mo. Cloth, $1.75.

The present work describes the methods employed in the extended development of photography of moving objects attained in the last few years, and shows the importance of such researches in mechanics and other departments of physics, the fine arts, physiology and zoölogy, and in regulating the walking or marching of men and the gait of horses.

RACE AND LANGUAGE. By ANDRÉ LEFÈVRE, Professor in the Anthropological School, Paris. 12mo. Cloth, $1.50.

"A most scholarly exposition of the evolution of language, and a comprehensive account of the Indo-European group of tongues."—*Boston Advertiser.*

"A welcome contribution to the study of the obscure and complicated subject with which it deals."—*San Francisco Chronicle.*

"One of the few scientific works which promise to become popular, both with those who read for instruction and those who read for recreation."—*Philadelphia Item.*

MAN AND THE GLACIAL PERIOD. By G. FREDERICK WRIGHT, D. D., LL. D., author of "The Ice Age in North America," "Logic of Christian Evidences," etc. With numerous Illustrations. 12mo. Cloth, $1.75.

"The author is himself an independent student and thinker, whose competence and authority are undisputed."—*New York Sun.*

"It may be described in a word as the best summary of scientific conclusions concerning the question of man's antiquity as affected by his known relations to geological time."—*Philadelphia Press.*

HANDBOOK OF GREEK AND LATIN PALÆOGRAPHY. By EDWARD MAUNDE THOMPSON, D. C. L., Principal Librarian of the British Museum. With numerous Illustrations. 12mo. Cloth, $2.00.

"Mr. Thompson, as principal librarian of the British Museum, has of course had very exceptional advantages for preparing his book. . . . Probably all teachers of the classics, as well as specialists in palæography, will find something of value in this systematic treatise upon a rather unusual and difficult study."—*Review of Reviews.*

"Covering as this volume does such a vast period of time, from the beginning of the alphabet and the ways of writing down to the seventeenth century, the wonder is how, within three hundred and thirty-three pages, so much that is of practical usefulness has been brought together."—*New York Times.*

New York: D. APPLETON & CO., 72 Fifth Avenue.

D. APPLETON & CO.'S PUBLICATIONS.

THE LIBRARY OF USEFUL STORIES.

Each book complete in itself. By writers of authority in their various spheres. 16mo. Cloth, 40 cents per volume.

"In the popularization of science no more effective work has been done than that which has been undertaken by the projector of The Library of Useful Stories."—*New York Sun.*

"Accurate, interesting, useful, handy, and attractive are all words that apply with unusual force to The Library of Useful Stories. It is one of the most sensible sets of books that any publisher has had the good judgment to offer to the public."—*Cincinnati Tribune.*

NOW READY.

THE STORY OF THE STARS. By G. F. CHAMBERS, F. R. A. S., author of "Handbook of Descriptive and Practical Astronomy," etc. With 24 Illustrations.

"One can here get a clear conception of the relative condition of the stars and constellations, and of the existent universe so far as it is disclosed to view. The author presents his wonderful and at times bewildering facts in a bright and cheery spirit that makes the book doubly attractive."—*Boston Home Journal.*

THE STORY OF "PRIMITIVE" MAN. By EDWARD CLODD, author of "The Story of Creation," etc.

"No candid person will deny that Mr. Clodd has come as near as any one at this time is likely to come to an authentic exposition of all the information hitherto gained regarding the earlier stages in the evolution of mankind."—*New York Sun.*

THE STORY OF THE PLANTS. By GRANT ALLEN, author of "Flowers and their Pedigrees," etc.

"As fascinating in style as a first-class story of fiction, and is a simple and clear exposition of plant life."—*Boston Home Journal.*

THE STORY OF THE EARTH. By H. G. SEELEY, F. R. S., Professor of Geography in King's College, London. With Illustrations.

"Thoroughly interesting, and it is doubtful if the fascinating story of the planet on which we live has been previously told so clearly and at the same time so comprehensively."—*Boston Advertiser.*

THE STORY OF THE SOLAR SYSTEM. By G. F. CHAMBERS, F. R. A. S.

IN PREPARATION.

THE STORY OF ELECTRICITY. By JOHN MUNRO, C. E.

THE STORY OF A PIECE OF COAL. By E. A. MARTIN.

New York: D. APPLETON & CO., 72 Fifth Avenue.

D. APPLETON & CO.'S PUBLICATIONS.

THE STORY OF THE WEST SERIES.
Edited by Ripley Hitchcock.

"There is a vast extent of territory lying between the Missouri River and the Pacific coast which has barely been skimmed over so far. That the conditions of life therein are undergoing changes little short of marvelous will be understood when one recalls the fact that the first white male child born in Kansas is still living there; and Kansas is by no means one of the newer States. Revolutionary indeed has been the upturning of the old condition of affairs, and little remains thereof, and less will remain as each year goes by, until presently there will be only tradition of the Sioux and Comanches, the cowboy life, the wild horse, and the antelope. Histories, many of them, have been written about the Western country alluded to, but most if not practically all by outsiders who knew not personally that life of kaleidoscopic allurement. But ere it shall have vanished forever we are likely to have truthful, complete, and charming portrayals of it produced by men who actually know the life and have the power to describe it."—*Henry Edward Rood, in The Mail and Express.*

NOW READY.

THE STORY OF THE INDIAN. By GEORGE BIRD GRINNELL, author of "Pawnee Hero Stories," "Blackfoot Lodge Tales," etc. 12mo. Cloth. Illustrated. $1.50.

"A valuable study of Indian life and character. . . . An attractive book, . . . in large part one in which Indians themselves might have written."—*New York Tribune.*

"Among the various books respecting the aborigines of America, Mr. Grinnell's easily takes a leading position. He takes the reader directly to the camp-fire and the council, and shows us the American Indian as he really is. . . . A book which will convey much interesting knowledge respecting a race which is now fast passing away."—*Boston Commercial Bulletin.*

"It must not be supposed that the volume is one only for scholars and libraries of reference. It is far more than that. While it is a true story, yet it is a story none the less abounding in picturesque description and charming anecdote. We regard it as a valuable contribution to American literature."—*N. Y. Mail and Express.*

"A most attractive book, which presents an admirable graphic picture of the actual Indian, whose home life, religious observances, amusements, together with the various phases of his devotion to war and the chase, and finally the effects of encroaching civilization, are delineated with a certainty and an absence of sentimentalism or hostile prejudice that impart a peculiar distinction to this eloquent story of a passing life."—*Buffalo Commercial.*

"No man is better qualified than Mr. Grinnell to introduce this series with the story of the original owner of the West, the North American Indian. Long acquaintance and association with the Indians, and membership in a tribe, combined with a high degree of literary ability and thorough education, has fitted the author to understand the red man and to present him fairly to others."—*New York Observer.*

IN PREPARATION.

The Story of the Mine. By CHARLES HOWARD SHINN.
The Story of the Trapper. By GILBERT PARKER.
The Story of the Explorer.
The Story of the Cowboy.
The Story of the Soldier.
The Story of the Railroad.

New York: D. APPLETON & CO., 72 Fifth Avenue.

www.ingramcontent.com/pod-product-compliance
Lightning Source LLC
Chambersburg PA
CBHW031826230426
43669CB00009B/1239